100 faces of East End

the politicians, philanthropists, thieves, murderers, artists, actors, singers, entrepreneurs, builders, architects, seers, eccentrics, writers, poets, soldiers, sailors, adventurers, sportspeople, composers, inventors and charlatans who built the East End of London

For Joe and Billy ...
history in the making

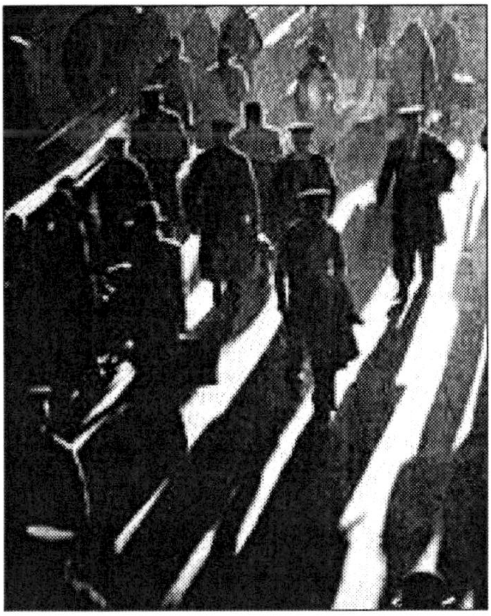

The features published within first appeared in the pages of East End Life, a weekly newspaper published by Tower Hamlets Council. These edited versions of the East End History page are republished here with the kind permission of Tower Hamlets Council. Thanks also go to the various editors of East End Life down the years, particularly to Laraine Clay, Patrick Kelly and Julian Scantlebury, and to assistant editor Helen Watson. Also, to Chris Lloyd of the Tower Hamlets Local History Library, and the various staff and members at the Ragged School Museum, the East London History Society, and the East London Family History Society.

Contents

Politicians, peacemakers and radicals 9
George Lansbury 10; Gandhi 12; Stalin 14; Jeremy Bentham 16; Errico Malatesta 18; Henry Bolingbroke 20; William Beveridge 22; Rudolf Rocker 24; Samuel Gompers 26; Thomas Cromwell 28; Sylvia Pankhurst 30.

Tricksters, thieves and killers 33
Fu Manchu 34; Henry Wainwright 36; Joseph Merceron 38; Jack Sheppard 40; Franz Muller 42; Samuel Dougal 44; Leon Beron 46; Jack Spot 48.

Stage, screen and cinema 51
Steven Berkoff 52; Sir David Lean 54; Lord Delfont 56; Charles Coborn 58; Richard Burbage 60; Jack Warner 62; Marie Lloyd 64; Reg Varney 66; Bernard Bresslaw 68; Lionel Bart 70.

Writers, poets and playwrights 73
Joseph Conrad 74; Wilkie Collins 76; Samuel Pepys 78; George Orwell 80; Daniel Farson 82; Matthew Arnold 84; Isaac Rosenberg 86; Charles Dickens 88; Israel Zangwill 90.

Seafarers, soldiers and adventurers 93
Sir Walter Raleigh 94, Captain James Cook 96, Jackie Cornwell 98, The Chinese General 100, Arthur Lovell 102.

Gentlemen, players and pugilists 105
Terry Spinks 106, King Cole 108, West Ham Utd 110, Harlem Globetrotters 112, Millwall FC 114, Doggett's Coat and Badge 116, Jack Broughton 118, East End boxers 120.

Contents

Priests, preachers and visionaries 123
John Wesley 124, Fred Charrington 126, Emmanuel Swedenborg 128, John Newton 130.

Musicians, composers and pop stars 133
Steve Marriott 134, Ronnie Scott 136, Peter Prelleur 138, Peter Green 140, Helen Shapiro 142, Wolf Mankewitz 144, Peter Grant 146, Billy Ocean 148, Jah Wobble 150.

Inventors, architects and pioneers 153
IK and Marc Brunel 154, Joseph Bazalgette 156, Sir Hugh Platt, 158, John Dollond 160, Eugenius Birch 162, Benjamin Gompertz 164, John Rennie166, Robert Hooke 168, Nicholas Hawksmoor 170

Eccentrics, mystics and charlatans 173
Joseph Druce 174, The Tichborne Claimant 176, Eliza Marchpane 178, The Blind Beggar 180; The Mad Hatter 182; Charlie Brown.

Designers, painters and photographers 187
The cockney photographers 188; Barber Beaumont 190; Mark Gertler 192; William Holman Hunt 194; John Edwards and Francis Bacon 196; William Larkins 198; CR Ashbee 200; Abram Games 202.

Philanthropists, doctors and scientists 205
Granville Sharp 206; Hannah Billig 208; Angela Burdett-Coutts 210; Tubby Clayton 212; George Peabody 214.

Entrepreneurs, industrialists, businessmen 217
Lew Grade 218; William Caslon 220; Thomas Frye 222; William Lusty 224; Sidney Bloom 226; Lesney 228.

Index 224

Introduction

The hundred or so characters covered within these pages first appeared weekly in *East End Life*, the weekly newspaper for the Tower Hamlets borough of east London. The brief was to find someone or something historically interesting to say about the East End on a weekly basis - oh and to do so in 700 words, no more no less. The first bit was easy: this part of London contains the docks, the Tower of London and is right next door to the City of London. Most importantly though, it was the first port of call for visitors to London for 2000 years, from the Romans and Boudicca, through waves of Irish, Jewish, German, Bangladeshi and, more recently, Somali immigration. Those wanting a new start, a new life or a new challenge stepped off the boat here and they've brought a thousand stories with them. Little wonder that the East End became a furnace of ideas, creativity in the arts, entrepreneurial flair and political radicalism ... very often, it happened here first. Unsurprisingly too, this quarter of London where poverty was always only as far away as the next payday, also became a stamping ground for thieves, murderers, charlatans and tricksters. Summing each up in 700 words has always proved a little trickier.

Some readers may frown over the classification of certain characters. Do we classify Lew Grade and Bernard Delfont under showbiz or as entrepreneurs? Were the Brunels inventors or businessmen? Where do we cross the line from religious visionary to eccentric or even charlatan? Sometimes it gets more difficult. Sir Walter Raleigh may be an adventurer to some, but a pirate and murderer to others. Sam Gompers was a hero of organised labour but fought equally hard to stop Chinese immigrants 'stealing' jobs. But many of these characters made their names and fortunes in days of different mores, before our more enlightened days of awareness on the issues of racism and sexism. We may disapprove of much of the behaviour of these characters, but I don't believe that's a reason to write them out of history. Readers can find many more of these pieces (some 600 or so at a recent count) at www.eastlondonhistory.com. The random nature of writing a piece each week means there is no theme as such, so the chapter headings are just one way of making some sense of this jumble of characters. But assembling the book it seemed to take on a structure of its own, as characters wandered in and out of each others stories – Churchill seems to be forever cropping up, as does Hitler and the Kray Brothers. And there are some pretty odd neighbours rubbing shoulders in these pages: Henry VIII and Steve Marriott, John Wesley and Lionel Bart, West Ham United and William Wilberforce – the sheer tumble and jumble of names says a lot about the richness of the East End's history.

A word is needed too about our terminology. Many cities have an East End, but it has a particularly precise meaning in London ... depending on who you ask. For our purposes it is the area bordered to the west by the City of London, south by the River Thames, east by the River Lea and north by the borough of Hackney. This area is commensurate with the current London borough of Tower Hamlets. Nearby areas, including Hackney, Newham, Dagenham and out into Essex, are referred to as east London. The 'City' is the square mile of the City of London – actually a tiny part of the modern London metropolis and largely unpopulated, it is the financial district of today's London. This is where the 'cockneys' originally came from – within the 'sound of Bow Bells' refers to St Mary le Bow Church in Cheapside, not the East End area of Bow.

John Rennie, June 2006
johnrennie@gmail.com

Politicians, peacemakers and radicals

George Lansbury 10; Gandhi 12; Stalin 14; Jeremy Bentham 16; Errico Malatesta 18; Henry Bolingbroke 20; William Beveridge 22; Rudolf Rocker 24; Samuel Gompers 26; Thomas Cromwell 28; Sylvia Pankhurst.

Politicians, Peacemakers and Radicals

Lansbury the loved politician

Historian AJP Taylor described George Lansbury as 'the most loveable figure in modern politics'. To the people of his Bow and Poplar constituency he was a hero, going to prison to defend his beliefs and his voters. Yet to others he was naive, seeing in Hitler a germ of Christian belief that could avert World War II, and continually missing out on political power because of his refusal to compromise his beliefs.

Lansbury was born in Suffolk, in 1859, and his family moved to the East End nine years later. He started work in an office at 11 but, after a year, returned to school until he was 14. A string of jobs followed — clerk, wholesale grocer and coffee bar assistant among them. He then started his own business as a contractor working for the Great Eastern Railway but the business failed and in 1884 Lansbury, now married with children, emigrated to Australia. The family couldn't settle, and the following year they returned to England, George beginning work at his father-in-law's timber merchants. Embittered by his experience — he felt the authorities had painted a falsely rosy picture of Australia — he started to explore politics.

In 1889 he joined the strike committee of that year's bitter London Dockers Strike, and in 1892 he established a branch of the Social Democratic Federation in Bow. Then came a move that foreshadowed 'Poplarism' 30 years later. In 1892 Lansbury was elected to the Board of Guardians who ran Poplar Workhouse.

George Lansbury

The traditional approach for guardians was to make poor relief as unpleasant as possible, the theory being that generosity would encourage people to rely on the workhouse. Lansbury and his colleagues decided to change the system from within. Over the next years conditions in Poplar Workhouse improved dramatically. They sent inmates to the Laindon Farm Colony, near Basildon, where unemployed men learned basic market gardening ... it got many back to work. But in 1906 Government ordered an inquiry into the 'waste' of funds.

After three tries, Lansbury got to Parliament in 1910, Labour MP for Bow & Bromley. In 1912, he drew attention to Suffragette prisoners by resigning his seat to fight a by-election on votes for women. He lost, and next year was jailed for his speeches in favour of Suffragettes. For ten years Lansbury was out of the Commons and focused on journalism, helping found the *Daily Herald* in 1911: the paper opposed Britain entering the First World War.

> "He was an evangelist rather than a tactician"

Then, in 1921 he became Mayor of Poplar. Defying government, the Council raised the rate to increase poor relief, Lansbury and most of the local council going to prison for four months for their stance. Lansbury was often at odds with Labour leaders. When Ramsay MacDonald formed a National Government in 1931 to combat Britain's economic crisis, Lansbury resigned to lead a Labour opposition. He would resign again, with a pacifist stance on the brewing World War II. His views led him to Berlin, and talks with Hitler, then Mussolini, both leading him to believe they would enter talks to avoid war.

Another East Ender succeeded Lansbury as Labour leader. Clem Attlee looked back on his predecessor in 1954. 'An evangelist rather than Parliamentary tactician. Yet during the years he led the small Party in the House he showed skill and leadership. A leading Tory described him as 'the ablest Opposition Leader I have ever known.'

Bloody end for man of peace

For one man, 1947 was the culmination of a lifetime's struggle against the dying days of empire. But his triumph was shortlived. As the New Year of 1948 was ushered in, he had only days left to live. The assassination of Mohandas Karamchand Ghandi on 30 January, 1948, also brought to an end the long association of the Mahatma, which means Great Soul, with the East End. In 1931, Gandhi visited London for the Round Table Conference, on changing the constitution of British-ruled India. The British Government, after years of resistance to his revolutionary ideas, was now talking to the Mahatma, and offered accommodation. But long friendship with Doris and Muriel Lester led him to accept their offer of accommodation at Kingsley Hall, in Bromley-by-Bow. He had 16 years to wait before his dream of a free India would come to pass ... but then he had already been waging peace on injustice for 50 years.

Born near Bombay in 1869, Gandhi was a son of the Hindu merchant caste: his well-to-do father had been prime minister of several small states, and Mohandas was married when he was just 13 years old. But convention couldn't hold him for long. When he was 19 he came to London to study, reading Law at University College. He got his first taste of prejudice as fellow students snubbed him because of the colour of his skin. The young Mohandas was forced to spend hours in his room, reading alone. But it was here that the seeds of his philosophy of non-violence

Mahatma Gandhi

were sown. He absorbed the ideas of Henry David Thoreau's *Civil Disobedience* and returned to India, determined to put them into practice.

Unsuccessful in Bombay, Gandhi went to South Africa to work and became the first 'coloured' lawyer to be admitted to the Supreme Court. He swiftly took up the cause of fellow Indians who had come to South Africa as labourers, only to find they were treated as inferiors – it backed up his experience of England and the caste system back home. In 1906, he put his peaceful revolution into effect, saying he would die before obeying an anti-Asian law. Thousands of fellow Indians joined him in civil disobedience and Gandhi was jailed twice. But through all his tribulations, Gandhi remained loyal to Britain, organising an ambulance corps for British troops in the First World War. Then, in 1914, the long final passage of his campaign began when he returned home to India. He was an inspiring figure and Indians followed him in their thousands as he campaigned for 'swaraj' (home rule)

> "Gandhi took up the offer of a home in the East End"

and vowed to unite all classes and religions, especially the Hindus and Muslims. He encouraged Indians to boycott British goods, courts and authority – his reward was a series of jail terms during the 20s and 30s.

World War Two came and the politically astute Gandhi demanded independence as the price for India supporting Britain; again, in 1942, he was jailed. But in 1947, the years of peaceful protest paid off as independence was won. To Gandhi's horror, the splitting of the subcontinent into Pakistan and India brought Hindu-Muslim riots. He met violence with peace: fasting until the Delhi rioters swore themselves to non-violence. On January 30, 1948, on his way to pray, Gandhi was killed by a Hindu infuriated by his success in bringing the religions together. It was an ironic end to a lifetime's quest for peace.

Politicians, Peacemakers and Radicals

When Stalin came to stay

When a young Stepney housewife answered a knock on her front door on March 5, 1953, she expected to find one of her friends or neighbours on the other side – maybe even her mum, who lived next door. But Golda Berk was in for a shock. Standing outside her tenement door in Jubilee Street were reporters from radio stations and newspapers, and not just from Fleet Street but all around the world. It was the culmination of an extraordinary story that united refugees from Russia a half century apart.

Golda Berk was born in the East End in 1923, the daughter of Louis Toubervitch. Louis had journeyed with his parents from the Ukrainian city of Kiev, just one of the hundreds of thousands of Jews who travelled from Russia and the East to the sanctuary of London. But what had brought the world's media to her doorstep was the death of one of the most powerful men on the planet. For the man, who would later be known as Joseph Stalin, had lodged at 75 Jubilee Street as a young political refugee 46 years before.

Iosif Vissarionovich Dzhugashvili, aka Stalin, was born on 21 December, 1879, in Gori, Georgia, the son of a cobbler. He was a cruel child. Schoolmates would relate how he would stone birds for fun and greet news of sickness among fellow pupils with a cold smile. Perhaps it was because of his own misfortunes. He was a sickly boy, badly scarred by smallpox and born with a crippled left arm. He stood only 5ft 4ins tall: throughout his life, the

Joseph Stalin

self-conscious dictator wore platform shoes. But Iosif was a bright boy and a hard worker, winning a scholarship to the Tblisi Academy. His first career, as an accountant, did not hold his interest. While a student, Iosif had been absorbing the revolutionary works of Karl Marx and became involved in the first stirrings of the Russian Revolution. These were dangerous times and Iosif was frequently on the run. He was arrested in 1902 and imprisoned for 18 months: after his sentence, Stalin was sentenced to three years' exile in Siberia. He escaped in 1904 and met Lenin for the first time the following year, at a Bolshevik conference in Finland. Then, like many Russian revolutionaries, he fetched up in London in 1907, living in a Jubilee Street tenement flat – which was to be the future home of Golda Berk.

By 1910, Iosif was back in Russia where, like many of the Communists, he adopted a nickname: 'Stalin', meaning 'The Steel One'. It was another seven years before the Tsar was finally overthrown in the October Revolution. Then Stalin's swift and bloody ascent

> "Classmates recalled the young Stalin as a cruel child"

to absolute control of the Soviet Union began. He ruthlessly suppressed dissent, murdered his rivals and resettled peasants thousands of miles from their homes. Stalin's major triumph was to halt the march of Hitler's armies, with his people's resolute stand at the siege of Leningrad and the Battle of Stalingrad.

After the war, Stalin became increasingly paranoid and physically weak. In 1953, he looked to be plotting another purge of Moscow's Jewish doctors.

But it was to be the last emergence of an anti-semitism that surfaced throughout his life. The dictator died suddenly on March 5, 1953. Nearly half a century later, Golda Berk has long since moved to a new flat in Waterview House, near Mile End Park. The Jubilee Street tenement which once had such a famous resident has long been demolished.

Politicians, Peacemakers and Radicals

Bentham present but not voting

Casual visitors to University College London (UCL), just down the road from Madame Tussaud's, are often taken aback as they spot what appears to be a dummy, sitting in a glass cabinet in the corner of the entrance hall. But this is no waxwork, rather the fully-clothed skeleton of the college's founder. These bones are only the last chapter in the extraordinary tale of an East End boy's remarkable life.

Jeremy Bentham was born in 1748 in Red Lion Street, Spitalfields, now part of Commercial Street. He was a precociously-talented boy, reading Latin at the age of three and going up to Oxford to study at just 12. His lawyer father hoped his talented son would follow in his footsteps, and Bentham did enter Lincoln's Inn, to practise as a barrister, at the age of just 15. But a straightforward career in the law was too narrow to contain the extraordinary and eccentric intellect of the young Bentham. He soon gave up his work to study chemistry and the physical sciences, developing his ideas as he travelled in Italy, Turkey and Russia. In those days, scholars did not specialise to the degree they do now – science, politics and philosophy were not the separate disciplines they later became – and the young Bentham soon turned his thinking to philosophy, the law and social policy.

Bentham's ideas came together in what became known as Utilitarianism, a philosophical theory based on the doctrine of the 'greatest happiness of the greatest number'. It was radical stuff

Jeremy Bentham

and had its real influence a generation on, through philosophers like John Stuart Mill and many of the law reforms of the Century, such as the Poor Law. And Bentham's renown in the field of social reform was such that in 1792 he was made an honorary fellow of the fledgling French Republic. What the French champions of *'Liberte, Egalite and Fraternite'* would have made of Bentham's Panopticon, though, is not recorded. This was Bentham's design for a prison with inmates under constant surveillance. The philosopher put forward the idea of extending this to workers, soldiers or students to 'coerce by means of observation'. He believed organisations would first be transformed as those spied on were stimulated to hard work through fear ... and in the next stage workers would adopt values of hard work and diligence. Unsurprisingly it never caught on. But Bentham's ideas did. By the time he died in 1832, his ideas were shaping what we now see as typical Victorian values.

"His skeleton was clothed, a wax head popped on top and his body put in a cabinet"

In his will, Bentham specified that his friends 'take the requisite and appropriate measures for the disposal and preservation of the several parts of my bodily frame'. His skeleton was to be clothed, a wax head was to be added and the body placed in a wooden cabinet. And he had his memorial in UCL, whose founders wanted to start an accessible university: one that did not exclude students on the basis of religion, wealth, race, or creed. Critics referred to it as the 'Godless university' but the sceptics were outlived by Bentham – or at least by some physical vestiges of Bentham.

The eccentric radical sits there to this day. Tradition has it that the body is wheeled into all important meetings of the UCL administration. And in the minutes of the meetings, the East Ender is always logged as 'present but not voting'.

Politicians, Peacemakers and Radicals

Malatesta and the anarchists

In the early years of the 20th century the press and Parliament were in a state of near panic about the anarchists of the East End. Three events thrust them into the public eye. The first was the Tottenham Outrage. On 23 January 1909, two Latvian refugees from the East End attacked a messenger carrying the wages for a Tottenham rubber factory. In the course of the struggle shots were fired and overheard at the nearby police station. A police chase ensued, and they ran the criminals to earth after a six-mile pursuit in which two people were killed and 27 injured.

Then, on the evening of 16 December 1910, a Houndsditch resident heard hammering coming from the jewellers next door. A group of Eastern European emigres (and anarchists) was tunnelling through a wall to the safe. Several unarmed constables responded. One, Bentley, was fatally shot as he entered the building. In an ensuing street battle, Constables Strongman, Choat and Tucker were killed by gunfire. Then, on New Year's Day 1911, came The Sidney Street Siege. Police sealed off a house supposedly hiding the rest of the Houndsditch gang. Home Secretary Winston Churchill personally directed operations, police marksman opened fire, the building went up in flames, and the bodies of two men, Svaars and Joseph, were pulled from the embers.

Those events took place against a backdrop of panic about the influence of foreign 'troublemakers' upon the East End. Churchill later described Peter the Painter (a semi-mythical fig-

Errico Malatesta

ure possibly involved in the siege) as 'one of those wild beasts who ... were to devour and ravage the Russian State and people'.

The bigger story was that revolutionary politicians of the left had been driven from Germany and Russia and sought refuge in the East End. On Whitechapel High Street, opposite the London Hospital, a hall played host to the fifth congress of the Russian Social Democratic Labour Party (which played a key role in the emergence of the Bolshevik Party in the later USSR). Stalin came to the East End and stayed in a hostel in Fieldgate Street, and Litvinov and Trotsky visited too. With Lenin visiting Whitechapel, all the key players of the Russian revolution visited Tower Hamlets in the years before the First World War. And with the crowned heads of Europe falling one by one to popular revolutions over the preceding decades (and most of the rest to go by World War II) it was perhaps unsurprising that Churchill and the police saw activities in the East End as a threat.

Much official interest focused on the Anarchists Club in Jubilee Street. Efforts were made to tie one of the most prominent members, Errico Malatesta, in with the Houndsditch Murders. Malatesta was an Italian anarchist who had been arrested in his home country at just 14, in 1867, for writing a letter to King Victor Emmanuel II, complaining about a local injustice. He found London a safe haven, but in 1900, Victor Emmanuel's successor, Umberto, was assassinated, and the police began watching Malatesta. By 1909, he was under arrest, along with Rudolf Rocker, on a charge of criminal libel. He escaped deportation when supporters organised a protest in Trafalgar Square.

Searching the Houndsditch crime scene, officers found a card bearing Malatesta's name. It was a red herring: months earlier, one of the thieves had contacted the Anarchists Club, and been introduced to Malatesta. The Italian anarchist was found innocent. Britain never did erupt in anarchy. The East End revolutionaries were to return to their own lands to overthrow the ruling classes ... and no threat to Crown and Parliament was to emerge from Tower Hamlets.

Politicians, Peacemakers and Radicals

Women, drink and religion

The East End has long been a home for outsiders and dissenters. As a maritime gateway to the world, it was the first port of call for new ideas, practices and philosophies from Europe and beyond. Just outside the City walls it was a home for those whose views clashed with King and Parliament.

Henry St John Bolingbroke, who made his home in Spital Square when it was a country retreat at the extreme north-east of London, was a font of ideas, political ambition and energy. A mass of contradictions, he was a man of God and a philosopher, but also famed for his fondness for women and drink. A staunch supporter of the ruling monarchy of Queen Anne and her successor George I, he also managed to support the Old Pretender (James III of England and VIII of Scotland) in between.

Bolingbroke was born in 1678 and, after his studies at Eton and Oxford, and the customary Grand Tour of Europe which moneyed young men of the day used as their finishing school, he returned to London in 1700 with his mind set on women and politics. He married the daughter of Sir Henry Winchcomb in 1700. But even by the double standards of the day, Bolingbroke's infidelities were too brazen to ignore, and the couple soon separated.

Bolingbroke entered parliament in 1701, and soon he was becoming as renowned for his oratory as he had been for his high living. He joined the Tory Party and by 1704 was secretary of state for war. At 30, his meteoric political career was suddenly

Henry Bolingbroke

checked. The Whigs came to power and Bolingbroke announced his intention to retire from the exhausting business of Parliament and devote himself to study. In truth, he was as active politically as ever, but now operating behind the scenes, using his enormous influence as Queen Anne's favourite counsellor. The Whigs fell in 1710 and Bolingbroke was made foreign secretary, moving to the House of Lords in 1712 as Viscount Bolingbroke.

He was increasingly mistrusted despite – or, perhaps, because of – his brilliant way with words. He was a master of intrigue, not only whispering in the ear of Queen Anne, but using the London Tory clubs and writers such as the great satirist Jonathan Swift to swing public opinion in favour of his policies. So skilful was his manipulation of Parliament, though, that he managed to conclude the Peace of Utrecht in 1713 – the Anglo-French-Spanish treaty which established the first balance of power between the ever-warring nations – against enormous public opposition.

In truth, the wheel of fortune was turning again for the great schemer. Henry foresaw a pro-Whig Hanoverian succeeding the now-ailing Anne and he began negotiations with the Old Pretender, replacing senior Whig army officers with Tories. Events overtook him. Anne died suddenly in 1714, George I came to the throne and impeached Bolingbroke for treason, and Henry fled to France, where he helped plan James's Jacobite rebellion. At the same time, he augmented his fortune by marrying the rich widow of the Marquis de Vilette. But whose side was he on? James dismissed him as an English spy, though in 1723, he slipped the new king a hefty bribe, buying himself a pardon.

Back in Spitalfields, Henry continued to influence from the shadows. His new political periodical, *The Craftsman*, sniped at the government of Robert Walpole. In later years, his writings became preoccupied with religion. He argued the existence of God, using philosophy and reasoning, but he was a furious opponent of organised religion and dismissive of the notion of God as a bearded heavenly figure. The young dissolute died in comfortable and pious old age at his chateau in France in 1751.

The roots of the Welfare State

In the years around the Second World War, two men living and working in the East End laid the plans for the system that would deliver a newer, fairer world for the homecoming servicemen and women. Economist William Beveridge, born in India in 1879 and educated at Charterhouse public school and then Oxford, was a child of privilege. In 1903 he came to live at Toynbee Hall, in Commercial Street, becoming sub-warden with responsibility for educational activities, and staying in the East End until 1906.

Beveridge's expertise in the employment and unemployment field market was formed when he became director of Labour Exchanges at the age of just 30. A long career as director of the London School of Economics and as master of University College, Oxford followed. But his years in academia never dimmed the memory of his early years in the East End, his first-hand experience of the horrors that faced the unemployed, and the failure of a system with no safety net. There had to be a better way. And when, during World War Two, the Government approached Beveridge for his ideas on a new system to sweep away the deprivation and want of the pre-war years, he set to work on a report on Social Insurance and Allied Services.

The Beveridge Report appeared in 1942 and caused a stir of excitement throughout Britain, with its outline of a comprehensive scheme of social insurance. Beveridge proposed that every-

Beveridge and Attlee

one would be covered; no-one would want for food, health care or a roof over their head just because they were poor or had lost their job. People at home and the returning troops were enthralled – at last this was the fairer world the British had hoped for.

Meanwhile, having steered the British through the darkest days of the Blitz, privation, shortages and six long years of war, prime minister Winston Churchill was expecting a mandate for five years of Conservative government in the election of 1945. There was a hunger for change in the country, though, and to the old guard's horror a new Labour government was swept to power, under leader Clement Attlee. Clem was just four years younger than Beveridge and, like the great economist, was educated at Oxford. Like him, his eyes were opened when he came to live in the East End. He lived first at Haileybury House, off Ben Jonson Road in Stepney, then in 1908 became secretary of Toynbee Hall, joining the Independent Labour Party in the same year.

The parallels with Beveridge didn't end there. In 1913, Attlee started lecturing at the London School of

"It was the fairer world the British had long dreamed of"

Economics, a career swiftly interrupted by service in the First World War. On his return, Attlee became mayor of Stepney and quickly rose through the political ranks – serving as MP for Limehouse from 1922 to 1950 and serving in the first two Labour governments, in 1924 and 1929. In 1935 he replaced George Lansbury as leader of the opposition Labour Party. And, in 1942, the very year Beveridge published his report, Attlee became deputy PM to Churchill in the government of national unity.

In 1945, the new government started the most radical programme of social reform ever, with the creation of the NHS and the Welfare State. The last shadows of the workhouse were swept away by two men who had seen the scourge of poverty at first hand ... their visions forged in the East End of the early 1900s.

Politicians, Peacemakers and Radicals

The Catholic, Yiddish, Liberal Anarchist

The England of the early 1900s was a country of rapid change. The old queen had died, the telephone, electric light and the motor car were revolutionising the face of the capital, and the First World War was about to change people's lives forever. But for many East Enders it must have seemed as if they were still mired in the Victorian era. Sweated labour, poor money and bad housing meant their lot had, if anything, worsened. Things were particularly bad for the Jews who worked in the rag trade. And it was to take the influence of a German immigrant to make a firm break with the past.

Rudolf Rocker was born in 1873 in Mainz, Germany. His Catholic parents died young, but they had already given Rocker the liberal views that would early on infect him with a passion for politics. After leaving his Catholic orphanage, Rocker became an apprentice bookmaker, spending his spare hours working for socialist parties. Rocker was soon expelled, though, for not following the party line – but already his readings were pulling him in the direction of anarchism. His interests were by now attracting the keen attention of the police, and in 1892 he fled to Paris to escape harassment. Like many revolutionaries of the time, he quickly moved on to England, where the authorities took a slightly more tolerant view of political activists. And so, in 1895, the German found himself living at 33 Dunstan House in Stepney Green. There he found a fertile ground for his ideas – a disaffected and exploited workforce. Rocker had by now learned Yiddish and lived as one of Mile End's Jewish community. He was a popular speaker in the East End, but he had something more permanent in mind. In 1906, his group took over the disused Salvation Army hall in Jubilee Street, Mile End, turning it into a social club. People from all sectors and creeds of the East End flocked to the centre, using its library and reading room – he had set up one of the first adult education centres.

Rocker's work was growing but he was not going unnoticed by the Government. His leadership of the garment and dock strikes of 1912 may have been his finest hour but, in 1914, for the authorities at least, he at last went too far. Rocker bitterly argued against both sides in the First World War and found himself imprisoned. Suspicion of foreigners was at its height and his *Worker's Friend* paper was suppressed. Most cruelly of all, the Jubilee Street centre was closed, and in 1918 Rocker was deported to Holland.

"Leading the dock strike, Rocker pushed the authorities too far"

His work wasn't over, though. Back in Germany he led the fight against a new threat, the Nazis. In growing danger from the new regime, Rocker had to flee Germany once again; this time to the United States. Rocker lived out his long life there, finally dying in 1958 in Crompond, New York. Along the way he had fallen out with some old friends by backing the Allies in World War Two, while remaining the most famous anarchist in a country where it was a dirty word. For a generation of East Enders, his greatest legacy would always be those few years of the Jubilee Street Club ... and the power he gave them to read, to learn and to change their lives forever.

Politicians, Peacemakers and Radicals

US union boss from Spitalfields

The East End was built by the industry and endeavour of generations of immigrants: Huguenots, Jews, Irish, Bangladeshis and more. But just as fascinating are tales of the youngsters who left the poverty of east London in search of a better life and made their fame and fortune abroad. One lad who was a product of both these tides of immigration was Samuel Gompers. Though born to a poor Dutch family in Spitalfields, he would go on to dominate US trade unionism for half a century.

Gompers was born in Tenter Street, Spitalfields, on 26 January, 1850. He got his education at the Jews' Free School in Bell Lane but his school days were shortlived. Young Sam was apprenticed to a shoemaker at the tender age of ten. He soon swapped trades, becoming apprenticed to a cigar maker at a wage of just one shilling (5p) a week. It was a humble start, but one that was to dictate his fate. Many people were emigrating to the New World in search of a better life and Samuel and his family decided to try their luck in America, boarding a ship to New York in 1863.

But if the Gompers were expecting a land of milk and honey upon arrival at Ellis Island, they were in for a shock. Life was tough in the slums of New York, swollen as they were by millions of immigrants in search of work. For the Gompers, descendants of Huguenot immigrants, it must have seemed like the Spitalfields story all over again. Young Sam, eager to take up his trade, found that there were few large cigar factories in the city. Instead,

Samuel Gompers

most of the work was done in thousands of sweatshops; often the workers rolled the cigars in their own tenement blocks. The echoes of the East End and its sweated match and garment workers were hard to ignore. By 1885, Gompers had become an expert at his trade and was working in one of the larger shops. And with trade unionism rising in power throughout the western world (back in the East End, the dockworkers and matchgirls were at last rising up against their appalling pay and conditions) Gompers realised collective action was the only way forward.

He was respected by his fellow workers, most of them Germans, and they elected him president of Cigar Makers Union Local 144 (his local branch). Unpaid organisers like Gompers fought furiously to keep the union together under attack from mechanisation and the flooding into New York of new immigrants, most of them from Bohemia in eastern Europe. This was only the start for Gompers, who realised that if more workers got together, they would grow stronger. In 1886, he was elected president of the new American Federation of Labor, a kind of TUC. Working out of a tiny shed, with his son as the office boy, Gompers laid the foundation for organised labour in the US. With a budget of $160, he described it as 'much work, little pay and very little honour!' Just four years later, the AFL had a quarter of a million members.

"Working from a shed, he recruited 250,000 members in four years"

For 38 years, with just one year out, Gompers headed up the AFL. His influence didn't end in the US, at the end of the First World War, he travelled to peace negotiations in Versailles, where he helped set up the International Labour Organisation, a worldwide TUC. Gompers died in Texas in 1924. Look around Tower Hamlets and you won't see a street named after him. But if you ever travel to Chicago, remember an East End lad made good with a visit to Gompers Park on the Northwest Side.

Henry VIII's hatchet man

Thomas Cromwell rose from humble beginnings as a Putney blacksmith's son to become the second most powerful man in England. Yet having overseen the first English 'revolution' from his home in Stepney Green, Henry VIII's right-hand man met the same fate as many courtiers of his time – the executioner's block on Tower Hill.

The young Cromwell gained his experience in the field, with his colourful early career in Europe as soldier, traveller and merchant. The details of this early life were, perhaps deliberately, obscure, but the smith's son had picked up an education on his travels. On his return to England in the 1510s, Cromwell began practising law. In 1514, at the age of 29, he became collector of revenue for Henry's Lord Chancellor, Cardinal Wolsey. Cromwell's success in squeezing money out of the monasteries to swell the king's coffers did not go unnoticed. When Wolsey fell from favour, in 1529, victim of his engineering of a costly war against France, Cromwell quietly moved into his old mentor's place. His power swiftly grew, as he became royal councillor in 1531, master of the jewels and the wards in 1532 and King's secretary in 1534.

Here began what many historians describe as Cromwell's revolution. The king needed a way out of his marriage problems but Rome was unhappy with another request from England's serial husband. Cromwell found the way out – drafting the 1533

Thomas Cromwell

Restraint of Appeals Act, banning Catherine of Aragon from appealing for the assistance of the Pope. In the process he established royal supremacy of the monarchy over the Church. The dissident Church of England was about to be born. In 1535 he became vicar-general and vice-gerent in spirituals and exercised the new royal powers over the Church. Working with Archbishop Cranmer, the zealous Cromwell set about radical reform of the clergy. The two set about the dissolution of the monasteries, using the skills Cromwell had gained under Cranmer to break the priests' power and further stock Henry's treasury with gold.

Then, in 1536, Cromwell once more took a hand in Henry's marital affairs, securing the demise of former friend and ally Ann Boleyn. Career always came before friendship for the master power-broker. As chancellor of the exchequer and lord privy seal, the many-talented Cromwell was now making his power felt in Parliament too, doing his own will as well as the King's and changing so many laws that the 1530s is sometimes referred to as the 'Tudor Revolution in Government'.

> "A dramatic fall from grace, ending on the block on Tower Hill"

In 1536, Cromwell and the King had a real revolution to contend with. In Lincolnshire, discontent with Henry's taxes saw a popular rising threaten to topple the Lord Chancellor. The master player finally came unstuck when he brokered the wedding with Anne of Cleves, in 1540. As the daughter of a powerful Protestant duke, Anne suited Cromwell's political and religious game plan. There was one problem – the King didn't fancy his fourth wife and, six months on, the marriage was annulled. Thomas seemed to survive even this, and was made 1st Earl of Essex that year. But his influence was shot and a plot by conservative churchmen and courtiers saw him arrested on trumped-up charges. Cromwell left his home, the Great Place, by St Dunstan's Church in Stepney, for the Tower of London.

The founders of feminism

Around the world every year, on 8 March, people celebrate International Women's Day, and the role brave individuals have played in advancing women's rights. Few people have played a greater part than Sylvia Pankhurst, who directed her campaign for suffrage from Bow. Pankhurst, along with family, friends and other members of the movement, spent ten years fighting her battle from her headquarters at 400 Old Ford Road, and she regarded the East End as a crucial element of her campaign. 'I regarded the rising of the East End as of utmost importance,' she said. 'The creation of a women's movement in that great abyss of poverty would be a call and a rallying cry to the rise of similar movements in all parts of the country.'

Sylvia Pankhurst was born in Manchester in 1882, the daughter of Richard and Emmeline, and younger sister to Christabel. She was educated at Manchester High School, winning a scholarship to the Royal College of Art in London. When she came to London, she became passionately interested in human rights and equality. This was fired by her politicised family and, along with her mother and sister Christabel, she helped set up the Women's Social and Political Union (WPSU) in 1903. The organisation sought full equality between women and men. Most of all, it demanded votes for women.

It's hard for people today to realise how threatening this movement was to the political establishment. In 1906, Sylvia served

Sylvia Pankhurst

the first of many prison sentences for taking part in non-violent demonstrations demanding the vote. By 1907, there was a split in the movement. Unlike her mother and sister, she felt the best way to campaign for women's rights was as part of the wider Labour movement and she had now befriended Keir Hardie, a key figure in the emerging Labour Party.

She focused her energies on the East End, founding the East London Federation of Suffragettes, and publishing *The Women's Dreadnought* newspaper. In 1911, she published *The History of the Women's Suffrage Movement*. In it she outlined her beliefs, based on non-violent protest; she fiercely opposed the arson campaign some suffragettes were waging. In the autumn of 1912 the old bakers' shop at No 198 Bow Road became the first WSPU shop. Sylvia astonished passers-by by hanging a huge sign there demanding 'Votes for Women'.

So began a pattern of arrest, release and arrest once more. During 1913 she would be detained at rallies and return weeks later to Bow, weakened by her hunger strikes, to be nursed back to health by her friends, Jessie Payne and her husband, at 28 Ford Road. None of this stopped Sylvia's activism. Her work in the East End went on for the next 10 years, as she opened a women's co-op factory in Grove Road and the Mothers Arms mother-and-baby clinic in Old Ford Road. The factory was resolutely practical in intent, allowing women to go out to work for a living wage, while providing a creche for the children.

Sylvia lived until 1960, spending her last years in Ethiopia. There she founded monthly paper the *Ethiopia Observer*. When she died, she received a state funeral in Addis Ababa. Perhaps the greatest tribute people can pay to her today is to use their vote, every time they have the chance.

> "The greatest tribute to Pankhurst is to never waste your right to vote"

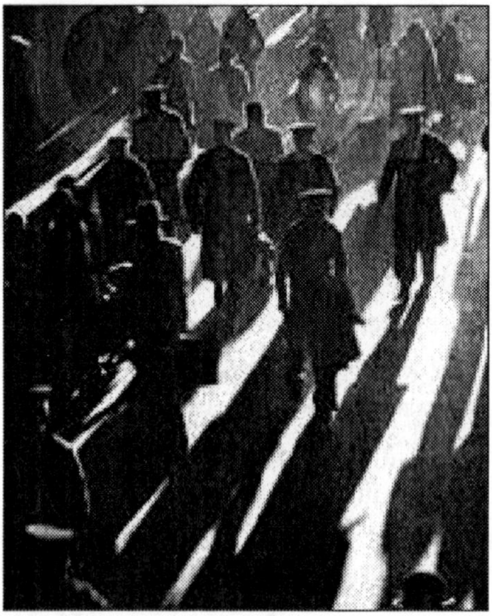

Tricksters, thieves and killers

Fu Manchu 34; Henry Wainwright 36; Joseph Merceron 38; Jack Sheppard 40; Franz Muller 42; Samuel Dougal 44; Leon Beron 46; Jack Spot 48.

Tricksters, Thieves and Killers

Fear, racism & the yellow peril

'Imagine a person, tall, lean and feline, high-shouldered, with a brow like Shakespeare and a face like Satan, a close-shaven skull, and long, magnetic eyes of the true cat-green. Invest him with all the cruel cunning of an entire Eastern race, accumulated in one giant intellect, with all the resources of science past and present, with all the resources, if you will, of a wealthy government ... which, however, already has denied all knowledge of his existence. Imagine that awful being, and you have a mental picture of Dr Fu-Manchu, the yellow peril incarnate in one man.'

When the reporter and novelist Sax Rohmer wrote those words 80 years ago he was obviously not doing much for the cause of racial tolerance. His portrayal of the evil criminal mastermind cynically tapped a strong vein of fear and mistrust of the Chinese community in the East End. And in the novels and Hollywood films that followed, Rohmer not only made the mysterious Dr Fu-Manchu a worldwide name, he gave fame to Limehouse ... the shadowy quarter from which the bad doctor sprung.

Rohmer first visited the East End in 1911, doing groundwork for a piece for the *Daily Sketch*. His brief was to discover the mysterious 'Mr King', a criminal boss who supposedly had tentacles in all the organised crime of the area but who had never been seen. Rohmer never found Mr King, but claimed that tucked away in the labyrinthine streets of old Limehouse, he had met Fu-

Sax Rohmer and Fu-Manchu

Manchu. That 'meeting' was to make his name and his fortune.

Myth, intrigue, and a fictional tradition was closely linked in the public's mind with Limehouse. The area had been a centre of barge and ship building for 500 years. And over those centuries, one of the East End's oldest villages built up a large 'Lascar' population. That was a catch-all term for the Asian seamen who, having worked a passage to London, were often paid off as soon as they hit port. Many worked their way back but many stayed.

Limehouse Chinatown got established around the 1860s and soon worked its way into popular fiction. Sherlock Holmes pursued his quarry here, and found rich young men slumming it in Limehouse opium dens. Oscar Wilde's Dorian Gray did the same and Hollywood producer DW Griffith travelled the area, researching *Broken Blossoms*. Victorian newspapers played it to the hilt, with reports of 'the yellow peril', of inscrutable orientals running their opium dens. Young white women were, supposedly, at risk of being drugged and spirited into the white slave trade.

Certainly, by the turn of the century, opium could be bought over the counter and was openly smoked, not just by locals but by the wealthy coming down from the West End to taste the mysteries of oriental Limehouse. During the First World War around 4,000 Chinese people were living in the East End but the numbers were soon to dwindle as fear of the visitors translated into an ugly backlash. Anti-Chinese riots broke out in 1919, as locals swallowed the yellow peril scare stories in the papers. The Government came down hard on the Chinese: hard labour then deportation was a typical sentence for possession of opium. Many were deported for far less, such as gambling on puck-apu.

In 1934, more brutal action was taken. The Council widened Limehouse Causeway, sweeping away the maze of houses and shops that gave the area its mystery. The Blitz did more damage – many Chinese names are on casualty lists from raids in 1940. The building of the Limehouse Link finally destroyed the atmosphere and topography of the old hamlet. The fog-bound labyrinth was swept away, and with it the ghosts of Chinatown.

Tricksters, Thieves and Killers

A middle-class murder in Bow

The life of a middle-class businessman in Victorian times had to be whiter than white. Of course, that didn't mean that all Victorians behaved with propriety. Behind many respectable front doors lurked violence, sexual licence and – in the case of Henry Wainwright – murder.

Wainwright seemed to be the epitome of hard-working Victorian respectability. He lived in style at 40 Tredegar Square, Bow, with his wife and four children, and ran a brushmaking business at 84 Whitechapel Road, with a warehouse opposite at number 215. Henry loved the theatre. The Pavilion was right next door to the brushworks and he often invited performers to Tredegar Square for dinner. Often, they would perform and recite in the Wainwrights' drawing room. However, his interest in the actresses went beyond the purely artistic, and he would entertain the younger, prettier ones at a succession of addresses around the East End. When he met pretty hatmaker Harriet Lane he decided to set up a lovenest for the two of them.

First he took an apartment at 70 St Peter's Street – the street is demolished today, but ran along the same course as the modern Warner Place. He then moved Harriet to the West End, before bringing her back to Stepney's Sidney Square. But Wainwright soon tired of his lover. Hoping to avoid fuss and scandal, he devised an elaborate plot to be rid of her, asking his brother Thomas to court her. To add to the confusion, Thomas adopted

Henry Wainwright

the curious pseudonym of Teddy Frieake – to the anger of the real owner of the name, an auctioneer friend of the Wainwrights.

What went wrong is uncertain. What is known is that Henry killed Harriet, battering her with a hammer and shooting her three times in the head. She was then interred in Henry's Whitechapel Road warehouse. Wainwright's life was rapidly falling apart. His business collapsed and he decided to leave Whitechapel Road for cheaper premises in Borough High Street. The only problem was Harriet. The stench of her decaying body was beginning to drift from the warehouse and into nearby Vine Court. Henry decided to take the evidence with him. He dug up the corpse, dismembered it and packed it neatly into paper parcels, even enlisting his employee, Alf Stokes, to help him lug them into Whitechapel Road. Wainwright left him guarding the parcels while he went to find a taxi. The suspicious Stokes sneaked a look in the top parcel and was appalled to uncover a human hand.

Wainwright took his cab. Flushed with the success of his plan, he even invited Alice Dash, a chorus girl at the nearby Pavilion Theatre, to share the ride to his new premises. Henry lit a cigar and the two set off for Borough, while the distraught Stokes ran behind, desperately trying to find a policeman to arrest the murderer. It wasn't until the procession reached Leadenhall Street that Stokes found a PC. Two coppers dismissed Alf's tale as the ravings of a madman, and it wasn't until the cab crossed London Bridge and entered Borough High Street that the warehouseman managed to persuade a pair of constables to stop the taxi.

The audacious Wainwright refused to open his parcels. 'Why do you interfere with me,' he demanded. 'I'm only going to see an old friend.' As the pair persisted, the desperate Wainwright said: 'Say nothing about this, ask no questions and here's £50 for each of you.' The officers opened the parcel to find the year-old parts of Harriet's body. Henry still protested his innocence, only recanting immediately before his hanging, even agreeing death was a fair sentence. Stokes received a £30 reward and set himself up in business, while Alice became lead dancer at the Pavilion.

Tricksters, Thieves and Killers

The thief who prospered

When the parents of Joseph Merceron settled in Brick Lane 200 years ago they wanted their son to follow in their Huguenot traditions and work in the silk trade – but young Joseph saw a much quicker way of getting rich.

London was growing fast at the end of the 18th century with businesses springing up and a whole new system of local government growing up to police and tax the new citizens. Money was flooding into London, but Merceron didn't set his sights on anything so crude as being a cutpurse or highwayman – he decided to use the system of law to his own ends.

Merceron started as a lowly clerk in a lottery office but quickly worked his way up to positions where he had power over money – other people's. Local government was based on the church parishes and Joseph, a slick and persuasive public speaker, won many friends and supporters at St Matthew's church vestry meetings. Parishioners voted the plausible Merceron into place as churchwarden, with control over funds for the needy, and of the lucrative licences for public houses. He had his start.

He shamelessly granted licences to friends, for a fee, of course, and a great many more were simply put into his own name. In his position as treasurer of the poor rate his abuses were even more breathtaking – cutting rates or increasing them, depending on whether the ratepayer was friend or enemy, while pocketing a cut.

Merceron was now also a magistrate, and lost no time in turn-

Joseph Merceron

ing that to his advantage. Although charged with keeping the peace, he encouraged bull-running and dog-fights in the streets of the East End, much to the delight of the locals who, as long as the magistrate got his percentage, now found that the law left them well alone.

Merceron greased enough palms to ensure he wasn't bothered by the authorities. With so many 'friends' benefiting from his patronage, Merceron seemed untouchable and Bethnal Green was seen as his personal kingdom. He thought he couldn't go wrong, and that was when Joseph pushed his luck too far.

In 1818 he was jailed for 18 months for stealing £1000 from public funds – a suspiciously lenient sentence at a time when men were hanged for far less. But his spell inside was just a hiccup in his successful criminal career.

While incarcerated, his prime enemy, the vicar of St Matthew's, mysteriously left the parish, probably scared off by the magistrate's henchmen, leaving Merceron a clear field on his release.

It was business as usual and Merceron even took up his old official duties, without any further interference from the authorities. Escaping the gibbet or the transportation ship, Joseph Merceron died a prosperous 75 in his Bethnal Green kingdom. Who says thieves don't prosper?

> "They buried him in his very own churchyard, remembered by a parish he spent his life defrauding"

Merceron left a few mementos of a lifetime of embezzlement and crookedness. Merceron Houses, Globe Road and Merceron Street, E1 bear his name. And his courtiers, mourning the man they hailed a hero, left an ironic testament to the appallingly corrupt magistrate They buried him in his own churchyard, St Matthew's, Bethnal Green, remembered by the parish he had spent so much time defrauding.

Tricksters, Thieves and Killers

The man they couldn't hold

Jack Sheppard was probably the most notorious and slippery East End villain of them all. Sheppard's fame lay not in the nature of his crimes – but in the inability of the authorities to keep him confined. Jack escaped from Newgate and other jails on no fewer than six occasions, making him one of the most celebrated anti-heroes of his day.

He was born in White's Row, Spitalfields in 1702 and was placed early in the Bishopsgate workhouse, before entering an apprenticeship with a carpenter. The indenture period was long – Jack served six years of his apprenticeship before cutting loose just ten months before his time was served. He immediately turned to thieving, and in 1724 was imprisoned in St Giles Roundhouse. Within three hours he was out, and the Sheppard legend began. He cut open the roof and lowered himself to the ground outside, using a rope he had fashioned from a sheet and blanket. He lost himself in the crowd and disappeared.

He surfaced again a few weeks later, lifted for pickpocketing in Leicester Fields – near present-day Leicester Square. Thrown into prison he was restrained with irons, but sawed through them, broke the chains and bored through an oak bar nine inches thick. Sheppard may have been a lousy thief, but his escapology was becoming almost supernatural, and the prison officers kept the broken pieces 'to testifie and preserve the memory of this extraordinary event and villain'.

Jack Sheppard

Jack was on the run for three months, before famed 'thief taker' Jonathan Wild ran him in. Sheppard went to Newgate, his sentence death. He was thrown into the condemned hold, but Sheppard had smuggled in a spike, and with it began boring through the wall. Accomplices were doing the same job on the other side, and soon he was free, mingling with the Bartholomew Fair holiday crowds, and escaping into the Smithfield streets.

He popped up again days later, robbing a watchmakers in Fleet Street. This time, back in Newgate, he was 'fastened to the floor with double fetters'. He had become a celebrated prisoner, and the wealthy came to view him in his cell. Sheppard in turn jibed and abused them. The anxious warders frisked Jack regularly, and finding a file that had been smuggled in, moved him to an even more secure cell within the jail.

He escaped, slipping his wrists through his cuffs. He used his chains to prise out a chimney brick and escaped to the room upstairs. It was a minute's work to spring the lock and, finding himself on the roof, he swung down to freedom, his blanket a rope.

> "He escaped again, slipping his wrists through his handcuffs"

He spent the next days lording it in London. Robbing a Drury Lane pawnbroker and hiring a coach and fine clothes with the spoils. Two weeks later he was back in custody. The 'most numerous croud of people that ever was seen in London' heard the judge sentence him to death a second time. He was to be hanged within the week, the authorities panicking that any longer and he would escape again. Though a penknife was confiscated from him on the way to the scaffold at Tyburn, his escapes were at an end. Sheppard swung. The legend continued however. A century later a report looked at the educational levels of East End children. Henry Mayhew's 1840 document noted that poor children 'who had never heard of Moses or Queen Victoria knew Jack Sheppard, the robber and prison breaker'.

Tricksters, Thieves and Killers

One-way ticket to murder

On 9 July, 1864, Thomas Briggs decided to travel on the new train line from Fenchurch Street to Hackney Wick. It was the worst decision of his life and also his last. Unluckily for 70-year-old Mr Briggs, his sole travelling companion was Franz Muller. Before their short trip was over both would enter the annals of criminal history. Muller was to commit the first-ever murder on a British train, while the unfortunate Thomas Briggs was to be the first victim.

When travellers boarded the train at the old Bow station, they found the carriage empty, save for a black bag, an expensive walking cane, a hat and a huge pool of blood. Briggs was discovered dying on the track between Hackney Wick and Bow. But of his assailant, there was no sign.

Muller, a 25-year-old German tailor, had failed financially in his homeland and again in London. He was now planning a new life in America. The gold watch and chain he had snatched from Mr Briggs' was to help pay for his ticket. It looked an impossible case, but Chief Inspector William Tanner of Scotland Yard thought differently.

The redoubtable Chief Inspector Tanner traced the stolen chain to a jeweller in Cheapside called John De'ath. De'ath remembered his customer – a young man with a German accent. The hat gave Tanner another clue. He knew it hadn't belonged to Briggs and the ace detective managed to trace it to a German tailor, one

Thomas Briggs & Franz Muller

Franz Muller. A search of the killer's lodgings revealed that he had made a hasty getaway, but Tanner was in luck again. A friend of Muller's at the lodging house told the policeman that the German was on board the passenger ship Victoria, steaming towards a new life in New York.

Chief Inspector Tanner and Sergeant George Clarke raced to Southampton and boarded the City of Manchester. The quicker ship reached New York two weeks before the Victoria and the pair simply had to sit back and wait for their quarry to arrive. The persistent pair found the gold watch in Muller's luggage along with Briggs' hat, which the killer had snatched by mistake as he fled the murder scene.

Muller's trial opened at the Old Bailey on 27 October, 1864. Mr Baron Martin presided and the Solicitor General, Sir Robert Collier, had the job of prosecuting the German. His counsel, Serjeant John Humffreys Parry, was a redoubtable defence lawyer but even he could not argue with the evidence of the Briggs Hat, which Muller had cut down by several inches in a vain attempt at disguising its appearance.

> "Boarding the Hackney Wick train was the worst decision of Briggs's life ... also the last"

In a bizarre and macabre twist, the hat's fame spread well beyond the Bailey. The new style became a fashion item and was adopted by fashionable young gentlemen of the day. His new role as a trendsetter was probably of little comfort to Muller. The jury found the evidence so compelling that they took just 15 minutes to reach a guilty verdict.

Muller was hanged on 14 November, 1864, but his fame didn't end there. Fears over the safety of single carriages were so great in the wake of the crime that the railway companies began to cut peepholes between compartments – and the new windows became known as 'Muller Lights.'

Tricksters, Thieves and Killers

The careless psychopath

Samuel Dougal was devoid of morals, a psychopath with no conscience and a murderer none to careful about covering his tracks. That he got away with murder for years was down to his unquenchable self-confidence and magnetic charm.

Dougal was born in Bow in 1846, finished school and secured a job as an apprentice in a civil engineer's office. But the young man was in search of fun, not regular work. When his debts, his drinking, his womanising and his father started to catch up with him, he ran off to join the Army, enlisting at Chatham in 1866.

For 21 years he toured the world with the Royal Engineers, in Wales, Ireland, Nova Scotia, and finishing his service at Aldershot in 1887, where he was quartermaster-sergeant and chief clerk. His army career was spotless but his home life was not so good. He married one Miss Griffiths in 1869. The couple had four children, but she had to endure his drunkenness and violence for 16 years. Then, in June 1885, she suddenly fell violently ill. 12 hours later she died in agony. Dougal returned to England on leave just two months later, with a new wife. In October she was dead, after a bout of violent vomiting. Both women were buried within 24 hours of death. And, as both died on military property, neither body was subject to post mortem.

In 1887, the regiment returned to England, Dougal with another woman, though this time they didn't marry. She had a baby, but was so beaten by Dougal she fled to Halifax, posing as a widow.

Samuel Dougal

The ex-soldier moved through a succession of jobs: publican, steward of a Conservative club, surveyor, clerk, salesman and storekeeper. There were even more women than jobs. He fathered two more children with a young widow, but again the violence was so much that she fled. He ran a pub in Ware, Hertfordshire, supported by an elderly woman and her cash. When the house 'accidentally' burned down in 1889, Dougal anticipated an insurance payday but wound up in St Albans Crown Court, charged with arson.

Dougal escaped due to lack of evidence and skipped off to Ireland, where he met and married Sarah White in 1892. The third Mrs Dougal bore him two children. By 1898, Dougal was without a wife again and his youngest child was dead after suffering from violent convulsions.

Camille Holland was a spinster of 55 when she had the misfortune to bump into Dougal at the Earl's Court Exhibition that year. She had recently come into an inheritance of £6,000. Dougal persuaded Miss Holland to invest in Moat House Farm, outside Saffron Walden, in January 1899. There was a succession of servant girls, most driven out by his drunken sexual advances. The last, Florrie Havies, was also the last person to see Camille Holland alive.

"He got away with murder for years ... on self-belief and charm"

On 19 May, Miss Holland said she was off to shop – her whereabouts would remain a mystery for four years. Dougal told Florrie her mistress had boarded a train to London and had written saying she would soon return. Remarkably, though rumours flourished, nobody chose to dig any deeper until April 1903. Then the police moved in to Moat House, digging up the farmyard and, on 27 April, Miss Holland's corpse was found in a drainage ditch.

The father of 11, husband of three and lover of many more was hanged at Chelmsford Gaol in Essex on July 8, 1903.

Tricksters, Thieves and Killers

Murder or assassination?

When the battered body of Leon Beron was discovered on Clapham Common on New Year's Day 1911, it was to set in motion the most notorious murder trial of the day. And it was to provide a day in court for some of the East End's most colourful characters... and least reliable witnesses. The case also dragged in the Home Secretary, Winston Churchill, plus allegations of spying and implications with the then-recent Sidney Street siege and Houndsditch Murders.

Slum landlord Beron wasn't universally loved. He owned nine decaying houses in Russell Court, Stepney, which provided him with 10 shillings a week, enough to pay his own two shillings rent on 133 Jubilee Street, Stepney, and provide the one and sixpence a day for meals at the Warsaw Kosher Restaurant at 32 Osborn Street, Whitechapel. It was at the Warsaw that Beron began to be seen in the company of Steinie Morrison, in December 1910. Morrison was another Russian Jew, who had arrived in England in 1898. Where he arrived from wasn't certain – he claimed to be Australian and also used the pseudonyms Alexander Petro-Pavloff, Morris Stein and Moses Tagger. What was certain was that he was a professional thief, who had served five sentences for burglary.

Beron was found in gorse bushes on the Common, his head staved in by a blunt instrument, his legs neatly crossed, his wallet emptied, and a curious 'S' mark carved into each cheek. They were, observed the police surgeon, 'like the f holes on a violin'. It took the police just seven days to pick up Morrison, arresting him as he tucked into his breakfast at Cohen's Restaurant, in Fieldgate Street.

They quickly discovered that he had been working at Lavender Hill, so might know the Common well. They also discovered that on the morning of New Year's Day, Morrison, using the pseudonym of Banman, had lodged a revolver and 45 bullets at the left luggage office of St Mary's Railway Station, in Whitechapel. They also learnt he had moved in with a Lambeth prostitute, Florrie Dellow, on 1 January – after telling his landlady that he was off to Paris. All very suspicious, but all circumstantial.

Defence and prosecution witnesses were as unreliable as each other: Beron's brother Solomon tried to hit defence counsel Edward Abinger when he implied he might have had something to do with Leon's death.

Abinger implied Beron was a police informant who had been assassinated for grassing on the anarchists responsible for the Houndsditch Murders and the Sidney Street siege. The 'S' marks stood for the Polish word 'spiccan' or spy, he suggested.

"Was it a common murder or an anarchist revenge killing?"

The policeman in charge, DI Wensley, scoffed at the theory, and the jury took 35 minutes to find Morrison guilty of murder. The judge had no option but to pass the death sentence, saying: 'May the Lord have mercy on your soul.' 'I decline such mercy!' shouted Morrison. 'I do not believe there is a God.'

The Court of Appeal upheld the conviction but the Home Secretary was not so sure. Churchill commuted Morrison's sentence to life. Ironically, it was a decision the prisoner himself would not accept. He repeatedly appealed to be put to death and, on 24 January, 1921, weakened by hunger strikes, he died in Parkhurst Prison.

Tricksters, Thieves and Killers

Crime king of Forties London

THERE have been some legendary figures at the head of East End gangland over the decades. From the mid-thirties to the mid-fifties the main man was Jack Spot, though like many others, much of his legend was self-penned.

Jacob Colmore, John Colmore, Jacob Comacho, Jack Comer - he was known by a multitude of names. But in a colourful age, (his rivals included Manchester Mike, Newcastle Ned and Edgware Sam) Jack Spot was his common title. He claimed it was because he was always on the spot when trouble needed sorting. More prosaically it was said to be a childhood alias given for the mole on his cheek.

Born on 12 April 1912 in Whitechapel's Myrdle Street, Spot was the son of Polish immigrants, his brother a tailor and his sister a dressmaker. But if his siblings took a predictable route for young immigrants, Spot was after better money. At 15 he became a bookie's runner, then a year later hooked up with a man running protection rackets on the Sunday morning stalls in Petticoat Lane. Times were tight, and the stallholders' main concern was to prevent new traders moving in and diluting their takings.

Quickly showing his aptitude for gangland, Spot managed to fall out with his senior partner, fought him, and took the protection business for himself, emerging as the self-styled 'King of Aldgate'. He went into partnership with East End bookie Dutch Barney, then took a more direct route – acting as lookout and

Jack Spot

minder to a successful housebreaker. Arrested and admitting to 40 offences, he was merely bound over. No doubt amazed by his luck, Spot went back to bookmaking. They say the bookie never loses: Spot made sure he didn't. If he had a bad day at the course he'd be off before the punters came to collect their winnings, and supplemented his takings with a fairground con called 'Take a Pick', where punters paid sixpence (2.5p) to pull a straw from a cup. Lucky winners (and there were few) won a piece of tat, while Spot pocketed £40 a day.

But a major part of the Jack Spot mythology centres on his protection of Jewish shopkeepers from the Blackshirts on their marches down Brick Lane. His status as friend and protector to East End Jews is certainly partly true – but he did charge the shopkeepers £10 a time. Nonetheless, it did the trick, and stallholders would be queueing up to donate money to the gangster's 'Market Traders Association', in fact just another protection racket.

He saw himself as 'the Robin Hood of the East End', travelling to Leeds, Manchester or Glasgow to beat up villains who threatened Jewish businesses. He even claimed that rabbis would advise their frightened people to call for his services.

> "Spot saw himself as a Robin Hood figure, but he always took his cut"

And he was still making a fortune from the races, meeting anyone who crossed him with instant and savage retribution. The White family, who had run betting at the major southern courses for years were harassed, attacked with knives, bottles, machetes and finally routed in a fight at Harringay Arena.

The date was 9 July 1947. Now in partnership with gangster Billy Hill, all serious opposition had been crushed. The two gang-leaders settled down as businessmen, living well on the proceeds of protection in West London.

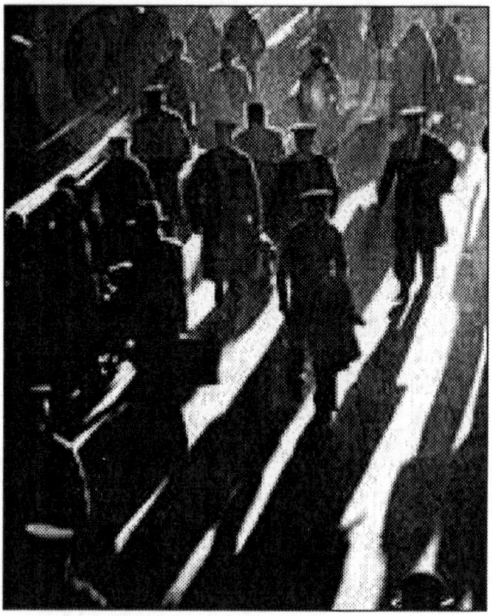

Stage, screen and cinema

Steven Berkoff 52; Sir David Lean 54; Lord Delfont 56;
Charles Coborn 58; Richard Burbage 60; Jack Warner 62;
Marie Lloyd 64; Reg Varney 66; Bernard Bresslaw 68;
Lionel Bart 70.

Stage, Screen and Cinema

An actor of many parts

You may know him as the suavely evil gangland boss Victor Maitland, who torments Eddie Murphy in the 1980s smash movie *Beverly Hills Cop*. Or the villainous Russian General Orlov, Roger Moore's adversary in *Octopussy*. You may know him better for his own plays, drawing deep on his childhood and teenage memories of East End life, to write and produce East and West. Or maybe as the producer and director of 30-odd years of avant garde theatre, bringing new life to the plays and books by literary heavyweights such as Kafka, with *The Trial* and *Metamorphosis*.

Steven Berkoff is a tough talent to pin down – which is probably just how he'd want it. His road to becoming an international movie star and successful director starts in the 1930s enclave of East End Jewish immigrants, and an endless succession of dead-end jobs. Berkoff was born in Stepney in 1937. Father Abraham (Al) ran a tailor's shop in Leman Street, from which the talented cutter would turn out lavishly-made zoot suits for the West Indians who were already settling in London. He also catered for East End boxers making a name for themselves – Jewish fighters like Ted Kid Lewis and Kid Berg, both world champions.

After the war, the Berkoffs returned to the East End following an ill-fated attempt to settle in the US. Home now was two rooms and an outside loo in Anthony Street, off the Commercial Road. With chickens in the back yard, it was a far cry from the glamour

Steven Berkoff

of New York, but there was plenty to entertain the young Steven. The Troxy Cinema in Poplar was the local venue for Saturday morning films, and there was the Palaseum at the end of the road for the Sunday afternoon film. Steven was enrolled at Raine's Foundation in Arbour Square, where he was a near-contemporary of playwright Harold Pinter. His physical welfare was taken care of by dips in the lido at Victoria Park in summer, and at Betts Street Baths, off Cable Street, in the winter.

The East End was a fascinating playground, and the young Berkoff would spend hours in Petticoat Lane market, transfixed by the wares at the stamp collectors' corner and examining the animals in the now-defunct Club Row livestock market for signs of ill-treatment. It was a world Berkoff would dip into time and again in his later work.

After a succession of aimless jobs in the fabric and garment trades, miserable stints in West End clothes shops, and a spell working in US Army PXs in Germany, Berkoff studied drama in London and Paris. He worked in rep,

> "He mixed avant garde theatre and Hollywood movies"

appearing on TV in 1960s favourites like *The Avengers*, before forming his own company, the London Theatre Group, in 1968.

Drawing on East End memories, Berkoff penned his first stage play, *East*, for the Edinburgh Festival in 1975. *West, Decadence, Greek, Kvetch, Acapulco, Sink the Belgrano, Sturm und Drang* and *Brighton Beach Scumbags* followed from the writer's prolific pen. Meanwhile, the energetic Berkoff was mounting plays in Japan, Germany and Los Angeles – *Richard II* and *Coriolanus* for the New York Shakespeare Festival – and touring his one-man show round the world. But to many he was better known for his film portrayals of heavies, revisiting the East End for his role as murder victim George Cornell in the film of *The Krays*. Recent appearances include Mr Wiltshire in the BBC's *Hotel Babylon* and lawyer Freddie Eccles in ITV's *Miss Marple*.

Stage, Screen and Cinema

A sense of direction

When Sir David Lean died in 1991, he left behind a huge home in Wapping and a reputation as a maker of some of the world's most famous films. *Lawrence of Arabia*, *Doctor Zhivago* and *Bridge Over The River Kwai* were big-budget, star-laden epics, and huge hits at the box office.

But it was a far cry from Lean's humble beginnings in the business – and if it had been down to his devoutly religious parents, the most successful director the British industry has ever seen would never have got on the set. The Croydon couple were strict Quakers who forbade the young David to go to the sinful cinema. He would sneak off from school to watch movies and dreamed of a career in films.

After throwing in an accountancy job, he became a clapper boy at Gainsborough studios. He swiftly moved to the editor's chair, cutting documentaries and production line B-movies. Noel Coward was at Gainsborough directing his first film and, with his keen eye for young talent, co-opted Lean to co-direct. It couldn't have gone better. *In Which We Serve* was a massive wartime hit, striking the right notes with a patriotic British public. Coward was a film and stage star, and Lean was a winning director.

A string of hits ensued. *Brief Encounter*, starring Celia Johnson and Trevor Howard, the Coward-scripted *Blithe Spirit* and *This Happy Breed*, followed by *Great Expectations*. In the Fifties, Lean continued his dual path – the romantic themes of

Sir David Lean

The Passionate Friends and *Summer Madness* and the patriotic harking back to the war years in *Bridge Over The River Kwai* and *Sound Barrier*.

Lean's huge hits of the Sixties relied as much on great writing as tight direction. *Doctor Zhivago*, shot in Spain and Finland, breathtakingly evoked the huge open spaces of the Russian Steppes, lasted nearly three and a half hours, cost a fortune and was the biggest hit of the mid-Sixties. It boasted the heavyweight talents of novelist Boris Pasternak and screenwriter Robert Bolt.

But perhaps the movie which will stand as Lean's masterwork was one made three years earlier and which, at 226 minutes, dwarfs even *Doctor Zhivago*. *Lawrence of Arabia*, starring Peter O'Toole as the British colonel leading an Arab revolt, broke the mould. 'Traditional movie storytelling raised to its highest form,' raved one critic. The audiences agreed and the film won seven Oscars, with best picture, best director, photography and score.

Ryan's Daughter, in 1970, didn't strike gold with the critics and the fans stayed away. Lean found himself out of fashion and it was difficult for him to finance the blockbusters which had been his trademark. He didn't make another film for 14 years. When he did, it was a triumphant return. *A Passage to India* in 1984 saw him writing as well as directing. It won five Oscar nominations, with Dame Peggy Ashcroft winning best supporting actress in her last film.

Lean was working on a film of *Nostromo* when he died – an adaptation of the novel by Joseph Conrad, who had made his home in Whitechapel a century before. Who knows what that union of East End minds, starring Marlon Brando and Paul Schofield might have produced? David Lean was married six times, divorced five, had one son, Peter, and died in April 1991.

> "Noel Coward drafted Lean in for his first directing job ... In Which We Serve"

Stage, Screen and Cinema

Boy who made the Grade

Three-year-old Boris Winogradsky stood bawling his eyes out. He was lost and a long way from home. To make things worse, he was trying to speak Russian to the confused PC trying to help him. It was 1909 and the scene was Brick Lane. His father Isaac arrived and, in fractured English, laid claim to young Boris. The family had journeyed across Europe, from the tiny Ukrainian town of Tokmak, via Hamburg and Tilbury, to make their home in Spitalfields. They weren't going to lose their youngest member that easily.

Baby Boris is better known today as Lord Delfont, part of Britain's most famed entertainment dynasty, theatrical impresario and producer of movies such as *The Deer Hunter* and *The Jazz Singer*. Most of it was down to hard work, persistence and ambition. The Winogradskys had left a simple life in Tokmak, 'centred on a house, a garden and some trees'. Now there was no house, no garden and no trees, just a room above a Brick Lane store. As mother Golda complained to Isaac 'Don't we deserve something better? Have we come all this way to live above a shop?'

It was the start of a perpetual drive to something better. A fortunate move to the still-new Boundary Estate soon followed. And Isaac supplemented his work in the garment trade by running a small (and unsuccessful) cinema in the Mile End Road. Meanwhile, he and his wife had a double act, singing Russian folk songs at the Mile End Pavilion, better known as the

Lord Delfont

Yiddisher Theatre, where there was always a sentimental audience for songs from back home.

By 1920, he was at Stepney Jewish School, and Barnet's habits got him into trouble. He was making a good living running a football sweepstake each week. So good was business that the young West Ham fan decided to up the ante by increasing the prize to sixpence. An eagle-eyed teacher called him to the front, and Barnet opened his hand to reveal a bunch of slips reading 'Chelsea, Tottenham Hotspur, Manchester United'. A caning and Barnet decided school was not for him. At 12 he never went back, and was soon to follow his big brother Lew Grade onto the stage.

First Barnet hit the London stage as an 'eccentric dancer'. A false start saw him reject his first job, in a revue's chorus line for famed producer Thomas Convery. 'I'm not accepting £3. I want £15 a week,' demanded the pushy Barnet. Thirty seconds later he was back out on Oxford Street.

In the Thirties, Bernie took the advice of old East End pal, tap dancer Keith Devon. 'You're a businessman, a natural. Why don't you go into management or set up as an agent?' By the late fifties, Delfont ran a stable of West End theatres, with agent brothers Lew and Leslie Grade supplying the acts. They'd hardly started though. Into the sixties and Lew was now in TV, as boss of ATV. It made sense for the new TV bosses to look to their variety background for talent, and Delfont's West End reviews would find themselves on screen. Bernie was now staging the Royal Variety Performance and reinventing London revue with the Talk of the Town.

Forced to retire as the boss of EMI because of his age, he set up First Leisure in his seventies, with nephew Michael Grade taking over. By now ennobled as Lord Delfont, the East End boy never slowed down until his death in 1994.

"At 12 he quit school and took to the stage ... there was no going back"

Stage, Screen and Cinema

Two lovely big hits for Coborn

There are plenty of East End streets named after famous ex-residents and notable characters, but there can't be too many that have given their names to celebrities. For Colin McCallum, an aspiring music hall performer of the late nineteenth century, it was a conversation with a pal on Bow's Coborn Road that led to a change of moniker. Something snappier was required for the theatre billboards and 'Charles Coborn' was born. His was to be one of the longest careers in music hall history, beginning with performances in the gas-lit Victorian halls of the 1870s, and ending with appearances in movies in the 1940s.

Remarkably, though Coborn's career stretched well into his nineties, his fame rested largely on two songs. McCallum came up with his first 'hit' himself. He wrote *Two Lovely Black Eyes* (or at least the music) in 1886 and premiered it at the Paragon Theatre in the Mile End Road. The Paragon, which sits on the site of the present Genesis Cinema at 93-95 Mile End Road, had only been open a year. This 'best ventilated theatre in London' (most were overcrowded, poorly ventilated and heavy with fumes from the gas lamps) was the premier music hall of its day, and the big crowds quickly caught on to Coborn's song.

He realised he had a success when walking through the streets of Bow. Gangs of youths would recognise the stage star and tunelessly bellow the chorus of 'Two lovely black eyes/Oh what a surprise/Only for telling a man he was wrong/Two lovely black

Charles Coborn

eyes'. Coborn wasn't annoyed, he knew he had a theme tune, and that people would pay to hear him sing it time and again. In the days before radio, TV or mass-produced recordings, canny artistes could make their material last for years ... and Coborn was to do just that.

There were many more numbers of course, largely the humorous or sentimental fodder of the Victorian music hall, such as *Should Husbands Work?* and *I've Loved Another Girl Since Then* but Coborn was to get another bite of the cherry with another hugely popular song. It was a close thing, he first rejected what was to become his trademark number.

In 1891, songwriter Fred Gilbert offered Coborn a ditty called *The Man Who Broke The Bank At Monte Carlo*. Coborn wasn't impressed and turned him down flat. But after spending a day unable to rid his brain of the chorus 'As I walk along the Bois de Boulogne/With an independent air/You can hear the girls declare/He must be a millionaire' he realised – with horror – his mistake.

> "He turned the song down, but couldn't get it out of his head"

Frantically, Coborn raced to track down Gilbert before he could offer the song to another performer. He paid the songwriter £10 for the rights and a whole new stage act was born. Coborn dressed and acted as an increasingly inebriated toff in his performances of the song. With each succeeding verse he would slur his words more and stagger around the stage. The punters loved it, raucously joining in on the choruses, and Coborn dined out on the song for years, eventually recording it several times up to the 1920s.

It seems a thin basis for a career by today's standards (or, looking at *X-Factor*, maybe not) but Coborn was still packing them in after nearly 70 years on stage. His final performance was a role in the British movie *Variety Jubilee* in 1943. Two years later, at the age of 93, Coborn died.

Stage, Screen and Cinema

The birth of London theatre

Whatever you think of Shoreditch, you're unlikely to consider it the heart of London's Theatreland. Yet, back in 1576, it was home to the capital's first playhouse. Throughout the Middle Ages, plays became hugely popular. But the actors, minstrels, jugglers and the like didn't perform inside. Instead, troupes would travel from town to town, taking the entertainment to a new audience every day.

They would perform religious mystery plays on church steps, the more ribald productions in inns and taverns. But the growing popularity of the more formal, many-act plays now being produced by the likes of William Shakespeare and Ben Jonson meant that cash could be spent on a permanent playhouse.

In 1576, the great tragic actor Richard Burbage, who was running his Lord Chamberlain's theatre company out of Shoreditch, raised the cash to build the capital's first proper theatre. The Theatre, as it was imaginatively dubbed, lay at the corner of New Inn Yard and what is now Great Eastern Street, and it was a huge success. William Shakespeare joined the company when he arrived in London in 1592 and, in the six years following, Shoreditch saw debuts of the Bard's earliest work – *Henry VI, Titus Andronicus, The Comedy of Errors, Romeo and Juliet* and many more.

The Theatre was demolished in 1598, its timbers taken to construct the world-famous Globe Theatre at Bankside, which was

Richard Burbage

uncovered again in the 1990s. But Shoreditch's theatrical story was just beginning. By now, Burbage's Curtain Theatre was doing a roaring trade at Holywell Lane, opposite the west end of Bethnal Green Road.

Shoreditch itself had started life as a religious, not a theatrical, hamlet. Like many villages it was born at the crossing of two Roman roads – in this case Kingsland Road and Old Street. First mentioned in 1148 as Scoredich, it was the site of the new St Leonard's Church in the 12th century, and in 1152 the Augustinian priory of Holywell.

But by the late 1500s, Holywell priory was gone and the theatre was built on its redundant grounds. Colourful characters began to replace the holy men who had sought sanctuary from the City. Many of the players are buried in St Leonard's churchyard. And in 1598, Ben Jonson fought a duel with Gabriel Spencer in Hoxton Fields, killing him. Spencer's body lies in the churchyard in Shoreditch High Street, with Burbage, and Henry VIII's jester, Will Sommers.

> "Shakespeare and Jonson invented the theatre in Shoreditch"

Around the 1680s, Shoreditch changed again. Most of the actors had migrated west and it became the focus for charitable works, as men made rich by the City looked to bequeath their wealth. In 1695, Robert Aske endowed the Haberdashers almshouses and a school in Pitfield Street. Then in 1715, London mayor Robert Geffrye built the Ironmongers almshouses in Kingsland Road – now the home of the Geffrye Museum.

By the 1850s, as London's population boomed, Shoreditch had a population of more than 100,000. Today, many people pass swiftly through this slightly scruffy north-west corner of the East End. But wander round St Leonard's churchyard and you can almost see the ghosts of Shakespeare, Jonson and the rest of London's first theatre community.

Stage, Screen and Cinema

The best loved copper on telly

Police dramas are one of the staples of our TV diet, with coppers tackling drugs, violence and murder as part of their daily routine. But long before *The Bill*, *A Touch of Frost*, *Inspector Morse* and the rest, an East End constable was dispensing justice and wisdom every Saturday night – and there was hardly a fight to be seen.

Beginning in 1955 and ending in 1976, *Dixon Of Dock Green* was (at the time) the longest-running police series on British television. Central character George Dixon was inseparable in the minds of the public from the man who played him: veteran East End actor Jack Warner. Warner was a pseudonym of course. He had actually been born Horace John Waters. His place of birth was 1 Rounton Road Bow in 1895. But by the time Horace was trying to make a name for himself as an actor, his sisters were famous, as the theatre and radio comedy and music act, Elsie and Doris Waters, and he had to adopt a stage name of this own.

Jack was to taste his greatest success later in life. He cornered the role of strict-but-fair father figure in a succession of post-World War II British films. An appearance in *Holiday Camp* in 1947 gave rise to a series of films featuring the Huggett family, with Jack as the head. He played his share of bad guys too, appearing as an embittered and heartless killer in *My Brother's Keeper* in 1948, and later as the secret boss of a criminal ring in *Hue and Cry*, a classic set among the bomb sites of the post-war

Jack Warner

East End. But it was his role as PC George Dixon in the 1949 Ealing Studios film *The Blue Lamp* which was to change Jack's life and career for ever. He played the East End policeman as a friendly uncle figure – and his death at the end of the film at the hands of a young thug, played by Dirk Bogarde, was not only tragic but deeply shocking for a British audience. Screenwriter Ted Willis revived Dixon for a stage play and then a series of six television plays. Little was he to know that he was soon to have a Dixon industry on his hands.

In *Dixon Of Dock Green*, Jack Warner was miraculously raised from the dead to play George Dixon once more – a widower raising an only daughter Mary (Billie Whitelaw in the early episodes, later Jeannette Hutchinson). Regulars included Sergeant Flint (Arthur Rigby), PC Andy Crawford (Peter Byrne), and Sergeant Grace Millard (Moira Mannon). In 1964 Dixon made sergeant.

Dixon focused less on crime and policing and more on the family-like nature of life in the station. And George Dixon, a warm, paternal and frequently moralising

"By the time he retired, PC Dixon was in his 70s"

presence, was the central focus. However as the 1960s and the early 1970s brought ever more realistic and violent police series from both sides of the Atlantic to the British public, *Dixon Of Dock Green* seemed increasingly out of touch. The Sweeney may have also been set in London, but it might as well have been in a different world, and a different decade. It was a trend towards coarseness and violence that the veteran actor loathed.

Altogether some 307 episodes were made, at first running 30 minutes and later clocking in at 45 minutes. And of course the early episodes were in black and white while the later ones were in colour. Falling viewing figures led the BBC to finally end the series in 1976. An affectionate public ignored the fact that (well into his seventies) Jack would have been retired from the Force for a good 30 years.

Stage, Screen and Cinema

The bawdy life of Marie Lloyd

The East End of the late 19th and early 20th century was the birthplace and home of music hall – and nobody personified the energy, bawdiness and vigour of the halls more than Marie Lloyd. The cockney chanteuse sang of drunkeness, lewd behaviour and moonlight flits. But musical fiction paled next to the facts of her outrageous life. It was a lifestyle that was to scandalise staid English society and would, ultimately, lead to her early death.

Matilda Victoria Wood was born on 12 February 1870 in Hoxton, the eldest of nine. All the sisters, Daisy, Alice, Rose and Marie, would hang around at the Eagle music hall round the corner: all wanted to go on the stage. The young Matilda had a taste for hard work and a flair for organisation. She cajoled her sisters and friends into group called the Fairy Bells Minstrels, who toured the mission halls with a programme on the evils of drink – ironic given Marie's later taste for the stuff. Although she was only 16, the determined Matilda announced she would go on the stage. Promoters were always scouting the halls for fresh talent and she soon got a try-out at Belmont's Sebright Hall in Hackney Road, and was then retained for a fee of 15/- (75p) a week.

Soon she was appearing at small halls around the East End, doing two or three shows a night, rushing from one to the other carrying her costume. Enormous success wasn't far away and it resulted from a potent mix of talent, ambition, relentless hard

64

Marie Lloyd

work ... and a ruthless and mercenary streak. Now dubbed Marie Lloyd she needed a signature song, and found it in *The Boy I Love Is Up In The Gallery*. She pinched the song from fellow performer Nelly Power and it quickly became her own, while Nelly faded from view.

Marie's career went into orbit. The audiences loved her and she loved the East End halls, where she constantly pushed the limits with her saucy winks, vulgarity and risque songs. Marie was such a huge star by now that she couldn't avoid the stories appearing about her in the papers. Eventually Marie had to appear before the Vigilance Committee, appalled by songs such as *She Sits Among the Cabbages and Peas*. She sang her songs without the usual winks and gestures and the committee let her go. Marie then gave a rendition of the chaste drawing-room ballad *Come into the Garden Maud*, so laden down with innuendo and gesture that it became quite obscene.

> "Her stage act was saucy, her private life scandalous"

In 1901 she began living with singer Alec Hurley. It was another shock for puritanical England – she wasn't to be divorced by Percy Courtenay till 1906. In 1910 Marie was 40, but sedate middle age didn't beckon. Instead she left Alec and moved in with Derby-winning Irish jockey Bernard Dillon, 18 years her junior. Her career began to falter too. In 1913 Marie and Bernard arrived in New York for a six-month tour. They were arrested at the quayside – their crime was to be unmarried. Charged with moral turpitude, they were deported straight back to Britain.

Marie began to drink. She often arrived late on stage, her voice became weaker and her act shorter. In October 1922 she was appearing at Edmonton and the last song in her act was the famous *It's a bit of a ruin that Cromwell knocked about*. The delighted audience howled at her staggering about on the stage, thinking she was acting the drunk. But it was Marie's final call.. Three days later, on 7 October, she died.

Stage, Screen and Cinema

Last laugh for the little clown

Reg Varney couldn't see too many avenues open to him when he left school. Comfortably the shortest kid in the class, at 14, the school leaver went to buy his first pair of long trousers only to find they didn't make them small enough.

Varney was born on 11 July 1916 in Canning Town, sandwiched in the middle of two sisters and two brothers. Things for tight for the Varneys. His dad returned from World War I to a wage of £2, 10 shillings (£2.50p) a week: a meagre wage, subsidised by mum taking in washing and keeping chickens. Star Lane Primary School didn't promise much better for Reg. Unable to get his head around arithmetic, he resigned himself to being the dunce of the class. An early ambition to study art was scuppered when he failed the academic section of the entrance test. Too tiny to take part in team games, even the weekly trip to the swimming baths was a trial; his heavy outsize costume would regularly end up at the bottom of the pool while a naked Reg swam round panic-stricken on the surface.

His size marked him down as ideal messenger boy material. Wearing his smart uniform, brass buttons gleaming, Reg would proudly board the No 15 bus from Canning Town to the City. The only problem was fighting his way through the adults to get onboard, and once on a seat, his feet were a long way from the floor. Unable to brace himself, he slid back and forth, all the way along the East India Dock Road, Commercial Road and into

Reg Varney

Aldgate. But Reg had other talents. One day, alone in the house, he found his dad's piano unlocked. He started to pick out tunes, remembering them from his parents' Saturday night parties. Reg never expected to get anywhere near a real theatre, but there was a thriving circuit of working men's clubs, and he soon won his first paid job, earning 8s 6d (42.5p) at Plumstead Radical Club in Woolwich. By the early thirties, Reg was earning £4 for a weekend's work – more than dad got for a week's labour.

There were some terrible gigs too. Playing at the notoriously tough Shoreditch Club, Reg watched in horror as the act before him, a bird impressionist, performed to complete silence. It was to feed the stage fright that would dog Varney for the rest of his career. During the thirties Reg worked non-stop, playing the clubs, singing with big bands and playing in cinemas during the interval – often to the complete indifference of the raucous, popcorn-chewing punters. A week's summer engagement at a 'classy' hotel in Southend turned sour. The hotel was a dive of a pub, Reg and his pal weren't paid, but the pair earned great money busking on the beach.

> "He was so small his feet dangled in mid air as he played the piano"

Reg enlisted for the Royal Electrical Engineers and, during World War II, he performed in Stars in Battledress and did a tour of the Far East. Although a fine pianist, his furiously energetic playing style combined with his tiny stature (often he was straining to reach the keys, feet dangling inches from the floor) always raised laughs too. Demobbed, he returned to Civvy Street and became an all round entertainer, working the music halls, with a young Benny Hill as his straight man. The pair were an early success on TV, debuting in 1947. But it was a show that first rolled out in 1969 that made him a household name. He starred as driver Stan Butler in *On the Buses*. The show ran for five years, seven series and 74 episodes, spawning three movie spin-offs.

Stage, Screen and Cinema

Gifted stooge of Carry Ons

WHEN king-size actor Bernard Bresslaw collapsed and died in June 1993, generations of Carry On fans mourned the loss of a giant comic talent. But his last role spoke volumes about the paradox of a well-read East End lad who could turn his hand to any role – yet was always cast as an amiable idiot.

Bresslaw was born in Stepney in 1934, the son of an impecunious tailor's cutter, himself a descendant of Jewish Polish immigrants. The young Bernie was a giant from birth, weighing in at 10lb 4oz and wearing size nine shoes before he hit his teens. The shoe size was a big disappointment to his mum – she wanted him to be a tap dancer. But Bresslaw had dreams of his own.

He could have followed his dad into the rag trade but instead was inspired by his English teacher, at Mile End's Coopers School, to chase his dream of acting. He applied to RADA, was accepted, and swiftly showed his potential in the Academy's performance of Christopher Fry's *Venus Observed*, not only winning the Academy's Emile Littler Award as Most Promising Actor but personal plaudits from the playwright himself. Bernard graduated and went into a notoriously tough form of rep – playing RAF and Army camps, Borstals and mental hospitals.

It was a tough baptism into the business but one that stood him in good stead. He later said that the demands of keeping happy the demanding all-male houses – who would soon let you know

Bernard Bresslaw

if you weren't up to scratch – was superb discipline and training for his later career. 'Like facing hostile fast bowling,' he laughed.

Bresslaw always prized his classical actor's schooling but it was a different sort of training that set him up for his big break. *The Army Game* ran from 1957 to 1962 becoming the BBC's top sitcom. Bresslaw drew on his National Service years as a driver/clerk in the Royal Army Service Corps to create the role of gormless giant Private Popeye Popplewell. Financial security, a spin-off film *I Only Arsked* and even a string of hits with pop singles followed – all with Bernie in character.

Bresslaw was a household name and his fame grew when, in 1965, he took on the first of 14 Carry On roles. Indian brave Little Heap in *Carry On Cowboy*, warrior Bungdit In in *Carry On Up The Khyber*, sinister butler Sockett in *Carry On Screaming* ... Bresslaw played them all while pursuing his classical career in the theatre. Roles in *Two Gentlemen of Verona*, *Much Ado About Nothing* and *A Midsummer Night's Dream* gave him artistic satisfaction in his work with the Royal Shakespeare Company, the Young Vic and the Chichester Festival Theatre.

"His act as a gormless berk concealed a marvellous talent for classical theatre"

But the heavy workload drove him to exhaustion and a collapse at a 1992 showbiz dinner. In the Eighties, virtual blindness threatened his career and his love of reading Racine, Milton and history. But a pioneering operation at Moorfields' Hospital saved his sight and he was back on stage. And it was there that the comic giant died – not as Bungdit In or Popeye but in the sort of role for which he craved recognition – waiting to go on stage as Grumio in the *Taming of the Shrew* at the open air theatre in Regent's Park. Bresslaw was married to dancer Betty Wright from 1959 until his death – the couple had three sons.

Stage, Screen and Cinema

Oliver's roots in the East End

Lionel Bart's music ranged from his greatest success, *Oliver!*, and musicals like *Lock Up Your Daughters* and *Blitz*. His songs such as *Living Doll*, *Rock With The Cavemen* and *Little White Bull* gave chart hits to British rock-'n'roll stars like Cliff Richard and Tommy Steele. It was a curious hybrid – but it had its roots in East End soil.

Bart was born Lionel Begleiter in Whitechapel in 1930, the 11th child of a Jewish tailor, and it was his childhood that formed his songs. '*Oliver!* was a strange marriage of the Jewish music of my barmitzvah and the street cries of my childhood,' he recalled. 'Fagin's music was like a Jewish mother hen clucking away!' It was a colourful background, but one Bart embellished further. Many of his friends talked of his constant rewriting of his childhood, a habit which drove the ghostwriters of his biography to complete despair.

Certainly, although he never learned to read or write music, there were early signs of musical ability. Aged six, one of the young Lionel's teachers told his father that the lad was a musical genius, and his proud dad bought him a violin. Lionel soon got bored with the discipline required and dropped his lessons. At 16, he decided his artistic future lay with painting, and won a scholarship to St Martin's School of Art. That didn't last either, though. He was expelled for 'mischievousness', but didn't regret leaving the lonely life of the artist in his garret. 'I like a good mob

Lionel Bart

working around me,' he explained, an esprit de corps that would be fulfilled in the huge musical productions that made his name.

One thing he did acquire during his studies was that name. His bus journey from Whitechapel to the West End every day took him past Barts Hospital, and Begleiter reinvented himself as Bart. After National Service, Bart set up in business with his RAF pal, John Gorman. With a borrowed £50, they started a printing firm in Hackney. But business was never Bart's forte – this was the man who later sold the million-spinning smash hit *Oliver!* for a paltry £15,000, and poured in £80,000 of his own cash in 1965 in a vain bid to save the flop musical *Twang!!*

Anyway, music was changing, with big bands giving way to rock'n'roll, and Bart was spending time up West, mixing with young hopefuls like Tommy Steele and Cliff Richard in Soho's 2 I's coffee bar. At the same time he was producing his first stage show, *Wally Pone of Soho*, which debuted at the Theatre Workshop in Stratford, he was banging out the hits for Britain's answers to Elvis. He said he wrote *Living Doll* in six minutes on a Sunday morning – twice as long as it took Cliff to sing it.

> "Brilliant my boy, said Noel Coward. But were you on drugs when you wrote it?"

Bart was hugely generous with his cash, a legacy, he reckoned, of his gambling father. 'I hated money. My attitude was to spend it as I got By 1972, Bart was bankrupt, with debts of £73,000, and a drink problem. What cash hadn't been ripped off by acquaintances had been poured into unsuccessful shows. Often, his pals saw the warning signs. His friend Noel Coward, reading the script of *Quasimodo*, remarked: 'Brilliant dear boy. But were you on drugs when you wrote it?' Theatre impresario Cameron Mackintosh worked on a revival of *Oliver!* in latter years: 'Of all the people in this business, Lionel is the least bitter man I've met. He regrets it, but he's never sour, never vindictive.'

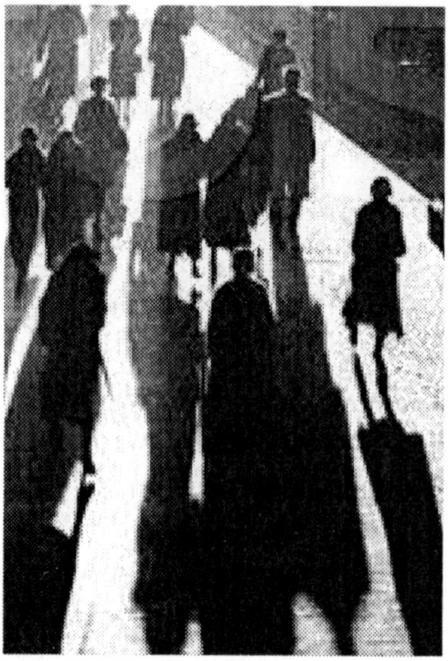

Writers, poets & playwrights

Joseph Conrad 74; Wilkie Collins 76; Samuel Pepys 78;
George Orwell 80; Daniel Farson 82; Matthew Arnold 84;
Isaac Rosenberg 86; Charles Dickens 88;
Israel Zangwill 90.

Writers, Poets and Playwrights

Conrad's heart of darkness

Many readers will know that the battle scenes for Stanley Kubrick's film *Full Metal Jacket* were shot not in war-torn Vietnam, but in the east London suburb of Beckton. But east London's connection with Vietnam-inspired Hollywood movies does not end with Stanley Kubrick's bloody epic.

For the greatest of them all, Francis Ford Coppola's *Apocalypse Now*, was born in the reminiscences and romance of an exiled Eastern European writer – as he gazed on the misty River Thames from his adopted East End home. Jozef Teodor Konrad Korzeniowski was born on 3 December, 1857, in Berdichev, in Russian-occupied Ukraine. His parents, Apollo and Evelina, were fierce Polish patriots and were swiftly exiled by the autocratic Tsarist regime. It was the first step in a journey that would take the young Jozef halfway round the world, before he settled in Whitechapel.

His parents died in exile, leaving Jozef an orphan. His uncle Thaddeus adopted the boy and, in 1874, conceded to his burning desire to go to sea. Jozef set off for Marseilles in search of a ship. Journeys round the world followed until, in 1878, Jozef joined a British merchantman, winning his Master's certificate. He got on well with his shipmates, quickly rising through the ranks. But Jozef's one problem was his name which, try as they might, the Englishmen just could not master.

Joseph Conrad

In frustration at hearing their tortuous attempts, Jozef decided if you can't beat them, join them, and changed his name to the more manageable Joseph Conrad. Suitably Anglicised, he decided to make his home in England. The East End was already a second home – he first stayed at the Sailors' Home and Red Ensign Club in Whitechapel, while serving on the Duke of Sutherland.

While he was on his long voyages, Conrad would while away the time by writing stories and, in 1885, he had his first success, when *The Black Mate* was published in *Titbits* magazine. In 1894, Conrad left the service, deciding to concentrate on writing. But his passion for the sea permeates his books. His journeys in and out of the Pool of London inspired the memorable opening scenes of *Heart of Darkness* which, almost a century later, Coppola would transform into *Apocalypse Now*. The book evokes a lost East End of bustling docks, sailors' flophouses and schooners waiting for the next high tide and fair wind. And the story unfolds from the cold, misty and lonely Thames Estuary to the final horror in Africa.

> "He passed the time on long sea voyages by penning ocean tales"

Many more novels followed, including *Lord Jim*, *Nostromo*, *Under Western Eyes* and *The Secret Agent* – ironically, Conrad came to be considered one of the greatest novelists in the English language, some achievement as it was his fourth tongue, after Russian, Polish and French. His was a colourful life but one touched by tragedy. In 1878, in a bout of depression, Conrad shot himself, but survived. His wife became an invalid and his son Borys was gassed in the trenches. But by the early 1920s, Conrad was a celebrated Englishman of letters. So English that in 1924 he was offered a knighthood – the naturalised Briton declined the honour. That year Jacob Epstein completed Conrad's bust. On 3 August 1924, Conrad died of a heart attack, and was buried at Canterbury Cathedral.

Writers, Poets and Playwrights

Bequest reveals life of scandal

In 1889, a strange bequest set up a 'people's library' at that home of East End culture and education, the People's Palace in Mile End. But the story of how the people got their store of improving literature is a strange tale of infidelity, false identities and Victorian morality.

Wilkie Collins was born in 1824, wrote 25 novels, more than 50 short stories, at least 15 plays, and more than 100 articles for newspapers and magazines. One of the superstars of Victorian fiction, Collins was a close friend of Charles Dickens, and like Dickens, Collins took a keen interest in the East End, visiting Tower Hamlets to research his books and pieces for newspapers. But while he was a celebrated man of letters, there was another side to his life, a side he had to keep hidden in sexually strait-laced Victorian London. For almost 20 years, Collins shared his private life with two women – and married neither. And to complicate matters further he had a home with each.

In 1854, when he was still a young and unknown writer, he met Caroline Graves, a 24-year-old widow with a young daughter called Elizabeth. It was a covert arrangement – they lived together, disguising Caroline's status behind the term 'housekeeper' – but it was one which lasted for the rest of Collins' life. Matters were complicated further when Wilkie met Martha Rudd in the mid-1860s. By now he was in early middle age, a famous and successful writer. She was just 20 and unmarried. But in the late

Wilkie Collins

1860s she moved to London and Collins set her up in her own home. The pair had three children and this domestic set-up was to remain for the rest of Martha's life. But the stigma of extra-marital sex could have destroyed Collins' career. With Martha, he assumed the character of William Dawson, barrister at law, and she became Mrs Dawson. The children were christened Dawson, and Collins lived in fear of their exposure, with the opprobrium that would bring. Two of his novels, *No Name* and *The Dead Secret*, deal with just that subject. He suffered terribly with arthritis too, taking opium to relieve the pain. It became an addiction, feeding the paranoid delusions that he used for material in his creepy classic *The Moonstone*.

Wilkie died successful and wealthy. But in an age when wives did not automatically inherit their husband's estate, his double life made things more complicated. Collins had planned for his death with the same precision he ran his double life though. His estate valued at £10,831, 11 shillings and threepence. Caroline and Martha got £200

> "He lived in terror of his children's illegitimacy being discovered"

each, the furniture in their respective homes, and each an annuity of £200 a year. On Caroline's death, the balance would go to Martha and her children. Sadly, and in a sinister echo of Collins's *The Woman In White*, daughter Elizabeth's unscrupulous husband, Henry Powell Bartley, made off with Caroline and Elizabeth's half of the estate. And when another daughter Harriet died, there was nothing left for Martha.

While he lived, Wilkie's will was a secret between himself and his lawyer. As soon as he died, the details were public property and an outraged Dean and Chapter of St Paul's refused to sanction a monument to the writer being erected in the cathedral. But the city's loss was the East End's gain. Collins spent his career trying to bring literature to working people and the £300 Collins had set aside for the statue instead set up the People's Library.

Writers, Poets and Playwrights

He wrote as London burned

Early on Sunday 2 September, 1666, the wholesale destruction of London began. A fire started in the house of Thomas Farynor, the king's baker, in Pudding Lane. Sparks from the burning bakehouse fell on hay and fodder in the yard of the Star Inn in Fish Street Hill and, just six hours later at 8am, fire was halfway across London Bridge.

The wooden buildings, stretching across the streets so their roofs almost touched, made ideal tinder for the fire. Five days later an area measuring one and a half miles by half a mile lay in ashes. 87 churches were razed along with 13,200 homes. The city that Shakespeare had known had gone for ever. But little of this would be known today were it not for the work of a Whitechapel woman's son, and for the safekeeping of the world's most famous diary in Bethnal Green at the height of the blaze.

Samuel Pepys had been born in Fleet Street in 1633, the son of local tailor John and Margaret, the sister of a Whitechapel butcher. During the English Civil War, Samuel was sent to the Huntingdon countryside, just as East End kids were evacuated during World War II centuries later. But he returned to London to study at St Paul's School. Coming down from Magdalene College, Cambridge, he entered the service of Edward Mountagu as his secretary and agent. Pepys was also building a career in naval administration, winning government posts and addressing the Commons on maritime matters.

Samuel Pepys

The year he started his diary, 1660, was a turbulent year. Charles II returned to the throne following Oliver Cromwell's death two years earlier, and our knowledge of Restoration Period England is largely down to Pepys. But it was his recording of the Great Fire that provides our most vivid image of the history of the time. He was one of the first on the scene and quickly hurried to Whitehall, returning with a royal warrant to allow houses to be demolished to create a fire break – Lord Mayor Bludworth had dithered, frightened that he would be held responsible for rebuilding costs.

As the fire spread, Pepys journeyed to Bethnall House in Bethnal Green, the home of his friend Sir William Ryder, and deposited his diary there for safe-keeping. The diaries ended in 1669, the year his wife Elizabeth died of a fever, and are only a brief snapshot of a long and successful career. The also graphically depict a London in the grip of the Great Plague, in the years before the Fire of London. Pepys went on to have two turns as Master of Trinity House in Stepney, a job as Secretary to the Admiralty, and he also became President of the Royal Society in 1684 and Member of Parliament for Harwich a year later. This ace administrator was to be the founding father of the modern Civil Service.

"**Pepys wrote his diaries in cypher. The code wasn't cracked until the year 1825**"

But by 1669, although only 36, the terrible headaches brought on by his writing and re-reading made Pepys fear he was going blind, and he closed the book forever. They might have been lost for good too, for Pepys wrote in an arcane code, perhaps fearful of political opponents. Amazingly, it wasn't until 1825 that the code was finally cracked, and it would be 1970 before the entire diaries were published. Pepys died on May 26 1703, aged 70, leaving no children. His only heirs were his diaries.

Writers, Poets and Playwrights

Down and out in the East End

Eric Arthur Blair was born in Bengal, the son of an Indian government official. He was educated at a Sussex prep school then Eton. His likely path in life was to follow his family's traditional steps into the colonial service or the Church of England. But Blair was to carve out quite a different career, as one of the 20th century's greatest writers. As George Orwell, he gained inspiration for much of his writing by weeks spent in a Poplar dosshouse.

Blair left Eton in 1921 and, instead of taking up a place at Oxbridge, returned to the sub-continent, joining the Imperial Indian Police. But after seven years in Burma he was growing restless. He found the climate unbearable, the health problems that were to dog the rest of his life had begun, and most of all he was starting to have severe misgivings about British rule in India.

His stirring political sense combined with his urge to write. And in 1928 he resigned, returning to Europe with the idea of writing about the urban poor. The next three years were spent among down-and-outs, first in Paris, then in London. Landing at Tilbury, the almost penniless Blair pawned his suit and made his way to a lodging house in Pennyfields, Poplar. It was an eye-opener for the young writer: 'Two or three of the lodgers were old age pensioners. Till meeting them I had never realised there are people in England who live on nothing but the old age pension of ten shillings [50p] a week.'

George Orwell

Blair spent his time with down-and-outs, compiling material for his journalism, talking to his fellow dossers ... or just killing time in the East End street. His overwhelming sense was of the boredom. 'All day I loafed in the streets, east as far as Wapping, west as far as Whitechapel. It was queer after Paris; everything was cleaner and quieter and drearier. One missed the scream of the trams and the noisy, festering life of the back streets.'

The people of the East End looked different too. 'The crowds were better dressed and the faces comelier and milder and more alike, without that fierce individuality and malice of the French. There was less drunkenness, and less dirt, and less quarrelling and more idling. Knots of men stood at the corners, underfed, but kept going by the tea-and-two slices [of bread and marge] that the Londoner swallows every two hours.' In Middlesex Street he watched amazed as a parent berated her child. 'What yer think I brought yer 'ere and bought y'a trumpet an' all? You little bastard, you shall enjoy yerself!' berated the mother.

"Life on the streets was a mix of poverty and boredom"

By 1932, Blair had had enough of the streetlife. His health wasn't good, and he took a job as a teacher. A year later, his diaries were published by Victor Gollancz as *Down and Out in Paris and London*. Fearing failure would hit his literary ambitions, the books came out under the pseudonym George Orwell. Orwell's reputation grew with *Burmese Days* and *Keep the Aspidistra Flying*, and a return to the horrors of poverty in *The Road to Wigan Pier*. Signing up to fight fascism in the Spanish Civil War, Orwell collected the material for *Homage to Catalonia*. He won huge success with the anti-totalitarian fable *Animal Farm*, in 1945, and retired to Jura in Scotland to pursue writing full time.

In 1949, he revisited the horrors of totalitarian government with *1984*. But his lungs, damaged by his years of rough living, failed on 21 January 1950, and Orwell died of tuberculosis.

Writers, Poets and Playwrights

A man out of step with life

Many an East End pub has a long and colourful history – the Blind Beggar as a haunt of the Krays, Bromley's Bun House with its widow's son legend, the Prospect of Whitby as one of the oldest Thameside houses. For one Island pub, fame was more fleeting. It came in the shape of a brush with royalty and the glitterati of Soho's art establishment.

In 1962, the Waterman's Arms was taken over by Daniel Farson. For a year or so it became a haunt of Princess Margaret, her husband Lord Snowdon, journalist Jeffery Bernard and top painters like Francis Bacon – all friends of photographer and TV presenter Farson. When Farson died a few years back, it ended a long and colourful life, fuelled by large quantities of booze and risky sexual encounters. In a career of heady excesses and expensive failures, the Waterman's Arms was one of the most costly.

Farson was born in 1927, the son of US journalist Negley Farson – an equally colourful character who would return from abroad with exotic gifts of elephants' teeth or Ashanti spears for his son. On one such expedition, the young Daniel was patted on the head by Adolf Hitler. Observing the boy's clean-cut good looks, the Furher approvingly ruffled his blond hair and called him a 'good Aryan boy'. 'He was as wrong about that as everything else,' Farson wryly observed in later years. For Farson never escaped the guilt he felt at his 'taint of homosexuality'.

Returning from wartime evacuation in Canada, Farson landed

82

Daniel Farson

his first job, as a lobby reporter at Westminster. He next ended up in the US Army, and discovered a passion for photography, shooting the ruins of the bombed-out Munich. Back in England, he followed his degree at Cambridge with a return to London. And it was in the Soho of the 1950s that he discovered the career and lifestyle that would make him famous – and often infamous.

In 1951, he joined *Picture Post* as a staff photographer. His spare hours were spent trawling Soho with friends like Bernard and Bacon. The morning after, Farson would appear with cuts and bruises after getting in a fight with a policeman or being mugged by a rent boy. By the 1960s he had moved to TV documentary. His work included *Living for Kicks*, *Farson's Guide To The British*, and *Out Of Step*.

The worst thing an alcoholic could do was take over a pub, but this was Farson's next venture, taking over the Waterman's Arms in 1962 and using it as a venue for old-time music hall. Friends such Princess Margaret came down to slum it, as West End toffs had done in East End music halls a century earlier. And the pub found fame when Farson made a documentary about its colourful characters. *Time Gentlemen Please!* gave the venture a brief boost, but the owner's boozing and lack of organisation meant it was doomed.

> "Boozers wouldn't imagine Princess Margaret sat here"

A year later, Farson sold up having lost £30,000 – an impossible fortune at the time. He retired to his parents' home in Devon, making periodic drunken forays back to Soho. In later years, Farson maintained his links with the East End, being an enthusiastic supporter of Whitechapel artists Gilbert and George. He was also an enthusiastic researcher into the myths surrounding Jack the Ripper. Of his Island adventure, all that remains is a much-changed Waterman's Arms – drinkers today probably never imagine they're sitting on the same bar stool that once supported the backside of royalty!

Writers, Poets and Playwrights

How poverty touched a poet

The Victorians loved their poetry, the longer, the more epic, the better. Tennyson and Browning fulfiled the need for lengthy verses (which father could recite to his attentive family on drawing room evenings) dealing with the great subjects of love, death and the lost golden age of England. But the third of Victorian poetry's 'Big Three' dealt with much more mundane, though no less important, themes – the misery and poverty that he had discovered as inspector of schools in the Bethnal Green of the 1850s.

Matthew Arnold was born into a life of solid respectability and educational excellence. He was the son of the renowned headmaster of Rugby public school, Dr Thomas Arnold. Arnold senior was passionately absorbed in educational reform, and his work was the model for the novel *Tom Brown's Schooldays*. Matthew was to continue his father's work, but not as a teacher to the sons of the rich. Like many mid-Victorians, the righteous Arnold felt that he had a mission to bring the improving medicine of education to the poor.

Schooling was the key to the working classes dragging themselves into 'respectability'. And where was in more need of education and respectability than London's East End? In 1851, he became an inspector of schools in Bethnal Green and his experiences provided fuel for his poetry. In 1867, he penned the poem *East London*. In it, he describes a summer walk through Bethnal

Matthew Arnold

Green and Spitalfields:
> *Twas August and the fierce sun overhead*
> *Smote on the squalid streets of Bethnal Green*
> *And the pale weaver, through his windows seen,*
> *In Spitalfields, looked thrice dispirited.'*

All poets have their big themes. Arnold wrote movingly on nature, the city and how men and nature were often crushed by the hustle and bustle of East End life. In *A Summer Night*, Arnold describes the men and women he sees as he goes about his day's work in Bethnal Green.

> *'For most men in a brazen prison live*
> *Where in the sun's hot eye,*
> *With heads bent o'er their toil, they languidly*
> *Their lives to some unmeaning taskwork give'*

Arnold also set down his thoughts in a long series of letters to Rosella Pitman, headmistress of Bethnal Green's Abbey Street School and sister of Isaac Pitman, inventor of shorthand.

This fascinating insight into Victorian thinking can be read at the local history libray in Bancroft Road, Bethnal Green, where it is still on display.

> **"All poets have their big themes. For Arnold it was how people were crushed by city life"**

Although Arnold was considered the third of the Victorian greats behind Tennyson and Browning, he anticipated that his turn would come, and later critics began to see him as perhaps the first 'modern' poet, particularly pointing to the nightmarish, irreligious world depticted in 1867's *Dover Beach*. With a fusion of the style of Wordsworth with modern, rationalist ideas, others have seen the writer as the first bridge between Romanticism and Modernism in poetry. And his *Essays in Criticism* inform the style of literary criticism to this day.

Writers, Poets and Playwrights

Whitechapel's own war poet

Today, the work of Wilfred Owen, Siegfried Sassoon and Rupert Brooke is widely read. But there was one who could have been the greatest World War I poet of all. The irony was that the war, having pulled the best work out of Isaac Rosenberg, would snuff out his life before he had the chance to enjoy the certain fame that awaited him.

Unlike the rest of the war poets, Rosenberg died a private soldier. The others were officers, children of comfortable, middle-class English homes. Isaac's story was very different. Rosenberg's family had fled Lithuania at the end of the 19th century, settling first in Bristol, where Isaac was born in 1890, then quickly moving on to the East End of London, lodging at 47 Cable Street. He was a pupil at St Paul's School, in Wellclose Square, Whitechapel, moving to Baker Street School in 1900, when the family moved to Stepney's Jubilee Street. Rosenberg was already showing a precocious talent for drawing and painting – Mr Usherwood, the headmaster at Baker Street, fixed up extra art classes for the lad at Stepney Green Art School. He was also showing skills at verse, composing poetry from age 14.

But unlike Owen and company, there was no public school and university in which to hone his skills – money had to be made. At 14, Isaac left school to take up an engraving apprenticeship at Carl Hentschel's firm in Fleet Street. It may have been a job, but the skills learned at Hentchel's and further developed at evening

Isaac Rosenberg

classes at Birkbeck College refined his drawing skills. At Birkbeck he won prizes for nudes in pencil and work in oils.

Rosenberg's life was running on parallel lines to that of fellow artist Mark Gertler – another artistic genius who blossomed from a poor, Jewish, East End family. And in 1911, just like Gertler, Rosenberg finally managed to study art full time, with a scholarship at the coveted Slade School. Also like Gertler, he suffered ill health throughout his life. In Rosenberg's case, lung problems brought on by the London smog led him to a rest cure first at Bournemouth, then in the healthy dry heat of South Africa.

In 1914, Rosenberg was recovering at his sister's home in Cape Town when he heard the news that war had broken out in Europe. Isaac was slowly finding success. A commission in July that year from Sir Herbert Stanley paid him £15 for one painting – £15 being the price of a ticket from Cape Town. He could have sat the war out but he set sail for London.

Gertler's most famous painting, *The Merry go Round* was an outsider's view of the meaningless madness of the Great

> **"He died leaving us to wonder what might have been"**

War. Rosenberg would view it at first hand. Most of the young artist's paintings were lost overboard in a storm in Cape Town harbour. And his luck seemed no better in London, where he applied unsuccessfully for a series of rent-paying jobs. But while struggling, he was finding renown as a poet as well as a painter.

He signed up in the army in 1915, but before going to the front he published a small volume of poems, *Youth*. Both TS Eliot and Ezra Pound admired Rosenberg's poetry and some say that, had he survived the war, he might have rivalled those two. He produced some of his greatest work in the long hours in the trenches. *Break of Day in the Trenches* and *Marching* compare with the best of Owen and Sassoon. But on April Fool's Day 1918, Private Rosenberg, 22311, 1st King's Own Royal Lancasters, was killed on dawn patrol.

Writers, Poets and Playwrights

Dickens' East End stories

If your idea of Christ-mas is mince pies, sleighbells in the snow, and a family feast round a roaring fire, then you're dreaming of a Dickensian Christmas. For all the elements of what we now think of a traditional Old English Yuletide were largely the invention of Charles Dickens, in his 1847 masterpiece *A Christmas Carol*. Ebenezer Scrooge huddles alone and miserable, hiding as a solitary youngster 'gnawed and mumbled by the hungry cold' sings *God Rest Ye Merry Gentlemen* through the old miser's keyhole. Throw in that other great Christmas invention of the Victorian era, the Christmas tree – imported from Germany by Prince Albert – and you have all the elements of an English festive season.

Dickens, of course, took as his source the people and places of London. And for Dickens, that meant the colourful characters and stories of the East End he visited as a child. His first encounter with 'this most colourful corner of the city' came with childhood visits to his godfather, Christopher Huffam, who lived in Church Row, which became Newell Street, in Limehouse. Dickens' childhood provided plenty of material for books such as *Oliver Twist*, with its hero cast out of a life of comfort and love into a horrific Thieves' Kitchen. In 1824, at the age of 12, Dickens' hapless father John lost his job as a clerk in the Naval Pay Office. He was swiftly imprisoned for debt, joined in Marshalsea Prison by his wife and children. With the exception of Charles that is. He was put to work in Warren's Blacking Factory. It only lasted a week, but the experience scarred him for life. And when he drew on it for *Oliver Twist* he also drew on his knowledge of the East End, placing the home of the evil Bill Sykes in Bethnal Green.

In 1829 Dickens became a reporter, and would spend the rest of his days dividing his time between a prodigious output of journalism, fiction and punishing lecture tours, with much of his work appearing under the pen name Boz. He continued to draw on his knowledge of the East End. Nicholas Nickleby's family inhabit 'a little cottage at Bow', an interesting historical snap of 19th Century rural Bow, before the new estates snaked out across the farmland from Bethnal Green and swallowed up the old village. David Copperfield has his first sight of London and stays at an Aldgate Inn. *Our Mutual Friend* pulls heavily on Limehouse as the home of many of the characters. And the Grapes pub, which stands in Narrow Street today, was used by Dickens as the model for The Six Jolly Fellowship Porters tavern.

"Happy childhood days were spent in Limehouse"

For his journalism too, Dickens returned again and again – journeys in Mile End, Wapping and Limehouse are detailed in *The Uncommercial Traveller*. Dickens workload took its toll and he died on 8 June, 1870, after a day's work on The *Mystery of Edwin Drood*. The unfinished last novel, researched in visits to the opium dens of Shadwell, appeared posthumously that September.

Dickens was buried in Westminster Abbey but his memorials were all around the East End. The hospital in Glamis Road, Shadwell, was financed by public contributions after Dickens' story of an East End in the throes of cholera appeared in *McMillan's Magazine*. And he is remembered by Charles Dickens House, Mansford Street, E2. But for most of us, his legacy is a Christmas of carol singers tramping through snow, and a family exchanging gifts around a roaring fire.

Writers, Poets and Playwrights

Fiction out of the melting pot

Jewish immigration to the East End produced a melting pot of businessmen, entrepreneurs, writers, artists and musicians. Among them was one writer who was unique – he not only grew up in the East End of East European Jews, he took it as the subject of his work. And in doing so he brought the story of the mass immigration to a much wider audience.

Israel Zangwill was born in 1864 at 10 Ebenezer Square, Stoney Lane, in the City of London – growing up in the streets off Brick Lane, living first in Fashion Street and then in Princes Street. Israel's father was a poor peddlar from the tiny country of Latvia, later to be swallowed up by the USSR. Israel was to make his fame by turning out a series of popular novels on the theme of immigrant Jews – in successive years *Children of the Ghetto* (1892), *Ghetto Tragedies* and *The King of Schnorrers*.

How he came from being the son of an impoverished immigrant to a successful writer was testament to the self-improvement ethic of the incoming Jews. Israel became a pupil at the Jews Free School in Bell Lane, Spitalfields, and then became a teacher. While teaching he set aside his evenings to study for a degree at London University, eventually passing his degree with triple honours.

And the energetic Zangwill was not content with work and study. While teaching in Bell Lane he was working on his first book, *Motza Kleis*, or *Matzo Balls*. This lively account of market

Israel Zangwill

days in Spitalfields brought him an enthusiastic and loyal audience – and Zangwill never looked back. Novels and plays followed, all richly observed slices of East End life. One of his most popular works was *The Big Bow Mystery*. A huge cast of characters knock against each other trying to solve the mystery behind the strange death of Oliver Constance, one of the most prolific orators of his day. Zangwill had a great flair for storytelling but, more than that, the mystery is a thoughtful satire of Victorian England, set 'in London's picturesque Bow district'.

But Israel's interests in the history and future of his people had long been leading him beyond fiction. He became a leading member of the Order of Ancient Maccabeans, a Zionist society established in 1891. The Zionist movement was working toward the establishment of a Jewish homeland, a dream that became reality with the birth of Israel in 1948. And When Zionist leader Theodor Herzl visited London in 1896 he met Israel to discuss the plans for that state. Argentina and Uruguay were two of the venues proposed for the new homeland, as well as the eventual Israel of the Holy Land.

"The Jewish East End served up lots of colourful material"

Zangwill attended the First Zionist Congress, supporting Herzl's Uganda Territory plan. It was rejected, and a defiant Zangwill led the 'Territorialists' out of the Zionist organization in 1905. He swiftly established the Jewish Territorialists Organisation (ITO) whose object was to acquire a Jewish homeland where possible.

Zangwill was never to see the setting up of Israel. He died in 1926, having laid much of the groundwork for his dream of a homeland – a future for the displaced Jews of Europe. But a visit to his books paints a rich picture of those people the century before, and of their long journey from eastern Europe to the new Promised Land.

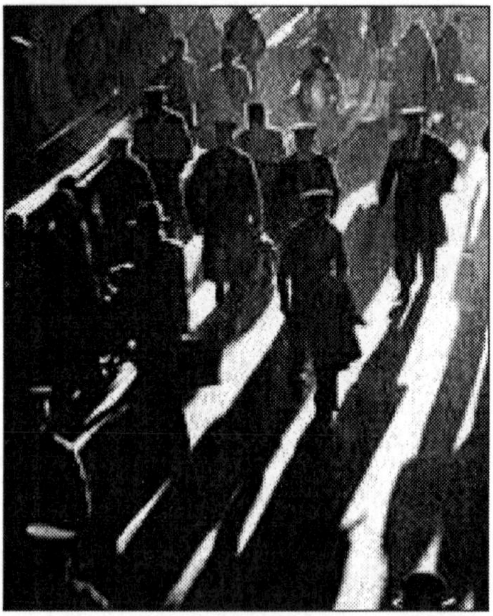

Seafarers, soldiers and adventurers

Sir Walter Raleigh 94, Captain James Cook 96, Jackie Cornwell 98, The Chinese General 100, Arthur Lovell 102.

Seafarers, soldiers and adventurers

Home from the ocean wave

Sir Walter Raleigh travelled the world in search of fame and fortune. But it was at opposite ends of what is now Tower Hamlets that the great adventurer had his two homes – though one was his choice and the other the King's.

He was born in Hayes Burton, Devon, probably in 1552. The Raleigh family were Protestant gentry: a dangerous status during the reign of Queen 'Bloody' Mary. Raleight developed a lifelong loathing of Catholicism – fortunately for him, Protestant Elizabeth I was soon to succeed her sister. After studying at Oriel College Oxford, the young Raleigh went to fight in the French civil wars between 1569 and 1572. Returning to England, the young adventurer found his first home in the East End. He lived in Blackwall, in a manor house that was finally demolished in 1890 to make way for the Blackwall Tunnel approach. Raleigh was a hero and became a prominent figure at Queen Elizabeth's court. He became a firm favourite of the Virgin Queen but, despite her insistence that Raleigh stay at court, adventure was in his blood. Overseas voyages and colonial ventures followed and he fought in Ireland in 1580-1.

Raleigh's sights were set farther afield and on greater fortunes, though. Humphrey Gilbert (Raleigh's half brother) had long had dreams of settling America. and found an eager backer in Raleigh. He set off in 1583 and annexed St John's in Newfoundland. The expedition left no settlers, though, and

94

Sir Walter Raleigh

Gilbert went down with his ship on the way back to England. Raleigh was ambitious to found a permanent colony and in 1585 led an expedition which established 600 settlers on Roanoke Island in Carolina, but a year later the colonists had to be evacuated. At home, things for Raleigh were no better. The Earl of Essex, Robert Devereux, was jealous of the adventurer's position at court and of his special place in the affections of the Queen. He set about undermining Raleigh, and his secret marriage to royal maid-of-honour Bess Throckmorton leaked out. The Queen was furious.

In 1595 Raleigh led an expedition to Guyana in search of Eldorado, the legendary hoard of gold that the Spaniards had long sought. Raleigh was unusually popular with the indigenous population, by all accounts, but the Queen was not so pleased. In 1603 the protection Raleigh enjoyed at court ended with the death of Elizabeth. Raleigh's attacks on the Spanish fleet had made him popular with the Queen, but the new king, James I, was determined to make peace with the Spaniards. In the same year it seemed Raleigh had outplayed his luck.

> "He spent 13 years in the Tower, writing a history of the world"

He was convicted as part of the Main Plot, the scheme to replace the king with Arabella Stewart. Sentenced to death, Raleigh found a second home in Tower Hamlets – the Tower of London.

For 13 years Raleigh lived under the threat of the executioner's blade. Never a man to lack ambition, he busied himself by writing his *History of the World*. He hadn't finished his magnum opus when fortune took an upturn. James released Raleigh for another attempt at finding Eldorado, but his skills as an explorer hadn't improved. All he found was Spaniards and a series of bloody clashes. It sealed his fate. He returned in 1618 to England and the executioner's axe. He hadn't found gold but is remembered as the man who (probably) brought tobacco and the potato to Europe.

Seafarers, soldiers and adventurers

Quaker roots of Captain Cook

Today we remember James Cook as the great explorer who 're-discovered' Australia and as an enlightened sea captain who turned the tide against the scurvy and vicious beatings that were the lot of the British sailor. We also remember Cook as a Yorkshireman, hailing from the beautiful coastal town of Whitby. But his life in Ratcliff and Wapping, and his association with the Quakers of the East End, may have played a large role in forging the captain's humanitarian approach to his men.

When Cook was born in the little North Yorkshire village of Marton on 27 October, 1728, his parents, James and Grace, could never have dreamt their son would rise to such fame. Cook's grandfather had moved to Yorkshire from Roxburgshire in Scotland, probably to work on the flourishing alum trade around the port of Whitby, whose boats in turn ran the goods down to the London docks.

James Cook Senior was a farm labourer who rose to become a manager – the expectation would have been that young James would follow in his father's steps. But after being sacked from his job as an assistant in a haberdashers shop, Cook signed up as an apprentice on the merchant ship of Captain John Walker. He was set to work on the regular runs of the merchantman Freelove as it hauled coal from Whitby to Wapping.

For a young sailor disembarking in the East End there were many temptations, all designed to relieve him of his pay as swift-

Captain Cook

ly as possible. In Shadwell and Wapping, every other house was a drinking den. Goods liberated from ships' cargoes were traded openly and the most likely job for a young girl was to become one of the thousands of prostitutes who worked the dockfront streets and taverns.

The pious and pacifist Quakers were very different and, despite persecution, had managed to establish a Friends meeting house in Wapping at the close of the 17th Century. Cook lodged with the Quakers and, in 1762, married Elizabeth Batts, one of their number. These connections may have played a key role in his developing an unusual compassion to his men and the 'natives' he encountered in his travels.

By this time, Cook had joined the Royal Navy and settled in the East End. His skill in navigation earned him swift promotion, rising from ordinary seaman to officer. He was responsible for the successful piloting of the fleet which took Quebec from the French in 1759. His part made Cook's reputation and he was chosen to captain the Endeavour on the Royal Society voyage to make astronomical observations from Tahiti.

> "Cook's sure touch deserted him in Tahiti where he was killed by locals"

Australia had been discovered by the Dutch in the early 1600s, but ignored by Europe since. Cook's journeys along Australia's eastern coast and New Zealand were epic but it was his insistence on lime juice, clean water, limited 'grog' and an improvement on the normal weevil-ridden ship's biscuit that kept his men alive. But in 1779, Cook's normally sure touch deserted him when he was killed by natives in Tahiti.

Elizabeth heard the news back in Wapping 11 months later. The church register of St Dunstan's in Stepney records the christening of several of the six Cook children, but in 17 years man and wife had spent a total of just four years together.

Seafarers, soldiers and adventurers

The boy hero of Scapa Flow

In September 1916, Britain was in the grip of the darkest days of the First World War. The East End in particular was suffering, with Zeppelin air raids razing houses and factories to the ground. Meanwhile, the carnage of trench warfare in Europe was cutting a swathe through London's youth. With men being slaughtered by the million, one more death might have gone unremarked. But the sacrifice of boy sailor Jack Cornwell caught the imagination of the nation – and earned a state funeral to rank with that of any monarch.

Jackie Cornwell was born in Leyton in January 1900. At 16, he would today have been finishing GCSEs and thinking about college. But in the Great War, 16 was old enough to go into battle. And, on the morning of 16 June, 1916, Boy (1st Class) John Travers Cornwell found himself on the deck of HMS Chester, joining the battle fleet at Scapa Flow. As the Chester picked her way through the morning fog, disaster struck. She had run into a scouting group of German destroyers. The British ship opened fire but the battle was hopelessly one-sided.

Three of the Chester's ten guns were knocked out in minutes, its crew lying dead or dying on deck. Despite sustaining terrible wounds, young Jack was the only member of his gun crew left alive. The losses were terrible, with 34 dead and 42 wounded – mainly casualties of the bomb splinters strafing off the water and along the deck. Yet despite his injuries and the horror around him,

Jackie Cornwell

Jack stood by his post. After the battle, he was transferred to Grimsby Hospital, where his condition deteriorated. Moments before he died, he called for the matron. 'Give my mother my love,' he told her. 'I know she is coming.'

His heroism was mentioned in dispatches by Vice-Admiral Sir David Beatty, who wrote: 'A report from the commanding officer of the Chester gives a splendid instance of devotion to duty. Boy (1st Class) John Travers Cornwell was mortally wounded early in the action. He nevertheless remained standing alone at a most exposed post, quietly awaiting orders till the end of the action, with the gun crew dead and wounded all around him. His age was under 16 and a half years. I regret that he has since died, but I recommend his case for special recognition in justice to his memory.'

The admiral would never have guessed just how publicly Jack was to be remembered. The dispatch appeared in the papers and, among all the millions of terrible deaths, Jack's story touched the hearts of the British public. More and more tales appeared in magazines and papers until, eventually, his mother bowed to public demand. She had Jack's body disinterred, and a public funeral was arranged.

> "The rest of the gun crew were dead, he was injured, but still Jack held his post"

On a baking summer's Saturday on 29 July, 1916, Jack's body was reinterred with full ceremony. The band of the Naval Volunteer Reserve led a huge group of servicemen, followed by a gun carriage bearing his coffin, covered with the Union flag. At Manor Park cemetery, the coffin was reinterred before thousands of hushed mourners. A fusillade of gunfire marked the end of the service and the band sounded *The Last Post*. On 15 September, Jack was recognised along with the other victims of Jutland – the brave boy sailor receiving a posthumous Victoria Cross.

Seafarers, soldiers and adventurers

Cohen the Chinese general

Morris Cohen was born in 1887, the son of Polish Jewish immigrants to the East End. His birthright was a life of devout religious piety and crushing poverty. Cohen soon gave up on studies, spending his time on the streets of Whitechapel, watching card sharps and the conmen working their pitches. In 1900 he was arrested for the first time, for picking pockets. He was sent to reform school and then, as was the custom in those days, shipped off to the Colonies – western Canada in Cohen's case. Shipping a 13-year-old boy halfway round the world with no prospect of ever seeing his family again seems a brutal remedy, but Cohen seemed to take to the rugged life of the Canadian wilds. He spent years wandering between Manitoba and British Columbia, building up a reputation as a hustler, a rabble-rouser and general troublemaker, with a taste for gambling and women.

Returning to the prairies after service in the Great War, Cohen went back to his card-sharping and con tricks at the carnies and fairs that travelled around western Canada. He became a regular customer at a Chinese gambling house in Saskatoon, where one evening he happened upon an armed robbery in progress. Cohen came to the aid of the Chinese owner – a brave deed in an age when the Chinese were considered fair targets.

Cohen now became lauded as a hero by the Chinese community and became interested in the volatile world of Chinese politics.

'Two-Gun' Cohen

The conflicting forces of Nationalism and Communism were soon to vye for leadership of that country, as its ancient imperial system teetered toward collapse.

In 1922, Cohen set off for China itself, signing up as a bodyguard for legendary political leader Sun Yat-sen. He became fascinated by Sun's ambitious plans to unify and develop China into a modern nation state. The stocky tough guy became a familiar figure at the leader's side, earning the soubriquet 'Two-Gun' as he always strode around with two enormous pistols at his hips.

Cohen was an aggressive and ambitious man, and his habit of talking up his own achievements saw him become an influential figure in Nationalist China. He became a friend and confidant to key figures in the revolution, and a general in the Chinese Army. The sharp-dealing Cohen was also building up a fortune as a property tycoon and arms dealer. He prospered in Asia while never learning a word of Chinese, but his career was halted with the Japanese occupation of Hong Kong. He was interned, and was to spend years in prison camps.

> "He rose from Whitechapel pickpocket to Chinese general"

He was released by the Japanese in 1943, sailing back to Canada and marrying Judith Clark. He regularly returned to China, treading a fine line between the two sides. The Nationalists and Communists were bitter enemies, China splitting into the tiny Nationalist-ruled Taiwan while Mao's Communists took control of the huge new People's Republic of China. Cohen professed loyalty, at various times, to both sides. Ageing, and with his savings gone on gambling and women, Cohen increasingly blurred fact and fiction, talking up his exploits to ever-greater heights. Picking through his extraordinary story, it's hard to separate his deeds from his dreams. His last visit to China was during the Cultural Revolution, as a guest of Zhouu Enlai. He died in Salford, England in 1970.

Seafarers, soldiers and adventurers

A hero in war and peacetime

Every November, the people of Britain wear poppies to mark the sacrifice of the millions of men and women who gave their lives in the Great War and other hostilities. Seventy or so years ago, the service at the Cenotaph was mirrored by services all over Britain – memories of the war were still fresh, and the silence was strictly observed. Traffic and trade would come to a halt as people stood in silence in the streets. As the two-minutes silence ended cars and lorries would roar back into life and people would go on their way.

For Limehouse costermonger Arthur Lovell, it was a miracle he found himself observing the silence at all. Arthur was one of the Old Contemptibles – he had volunteered to fight and gone out with the first battalions in 1914. Amazingly, among the carnage of the trenches, he had survived to finish the war at Mons on Armistice Day. Wounded twice, both times he returned to his company to fight.

On the morning of 11 November 1928, Arthur was observing the 'Great Silence' at his costermongers barrow in Burgess Street, Limehouse – in those days, the service was held on the actual anniversary rather than the nearest Sunday. As the silence came to an end, the horrified veteran saw a four-year-old girl, Rosie Wales, run into the busy road – right into the path of a steam lorry. Rosie faced certain death, and Arthur ran into the road, pushing her to safety. But the brave ex-soldier, who had

Arthur Lovell

cheated bombs and snipers' bullets for four years, slipped and was killed by the truck.

It was an act of heroism which caught the imagination of the nation. A week later Arthur was given a full military funeral – the crowds which jammed the streets of the East End dwarfed even those which had turned out for Armistice Day a week before. And the story didn't end there. At the funeral, the Bishop of Stepney told a strange tale from the days after Arthur's death.

'Last night there came to his house', said the bishop, 'a man who had been attracted by the name and asked if he could see the body. The man, looked, paused and then said quietly: "I thought so. This man saved my life in France during the war. I have not seen him since until tonight."'

The service was organised by the Rev CH Lancaster, chaplain of the 17th London Regiment, and he went on to tell the story behind this strange tale. Arthur had saved the visitor's life during a gas attack by lending him his gas mask, risking his life for a comrade. Again, he had shown not just an almost reckless bravery, but an uncanny ability to cheat certain death – almost to the last.

> "The Old Contemptible served from the earliest days of World War I"

Arthur was buried with full military honours and thousands lined the route, bringing the traffic to a halt once again. At the scene of his death, the gun carriage, bearing his coffin, came to a halt, and a wreath was brought forward. Then the carriage went on, followed by a costermonger's cart organised by Arthur's mates and piled high with chrysanthemums, orchids and, most poignantly, poppies. East End costermongers joined with Countess Haig to honour their hero and the service ended as little Rosie Wales presented a bouquet to the countess at Bromley Public Hall. Among the mourners were Arthur's wife and seven kids. Their dad had been a hero in peace as well as wartime.

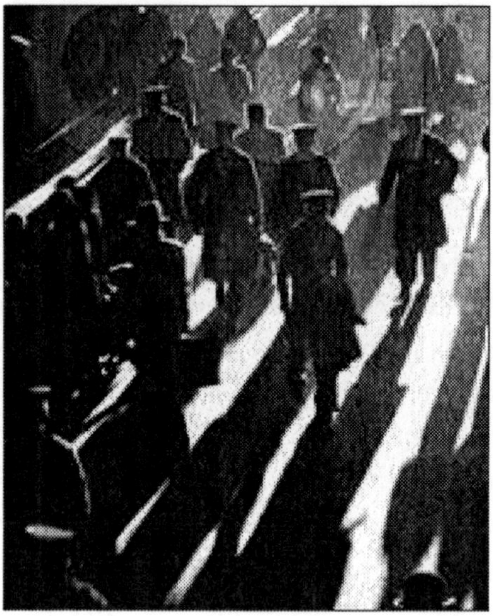

Gentlemen, players and pugilists

Harlem Globetrotters 112, Millwall FC 114, Doggett's Coat and Badge 116, Jack Broughton 118, East End boxers 120.

The baby-faced hero of the ring

As east London continues preparations for the 2012 Olympics, the thoughts of one East End hero will be racing back 44 years to another Games, and a precious gold medal. Terry Spinks was the babyfaced boxing hero of the 1956 Games in Melbourne. Just 18 when he boarded the plane for the Olympics, he looked ten years younger, but the unrumpled boyish features belied courage and skill beyond his years.

Gold medals are always hard to come by, but in 1956, the British fight game was on a starvation diet. Thirty-two long years had passed since a UK fighter had come out on top in an Olympiad, and Terry nearly didn't make the cut. It was a late call-up to the team – just days before, Terry had been emptying bins in Albert Docks. But he'd kept himself fit and ready, and he got the call he'd been praying for while he was training in his West Ham gym.

The flyweight had to win four fights before he made the final, against the Romanian champ Mircea Dobrescu. A mix of speed, skill and all the power his eight-stone frame could summon up saw Terry lift the gold, as fellow Olympic champions Gillian Sheen, Judy Grinham and Chris Brasher looked on. Back home, Canning Town was awash in Union Jacks, and the Spinks family were the surprised and delighted recipients of a case of Champagne, sent by Prince Philip. The rarity of the moment made it all the more precious.

Terry Spinks

Terry was joined by Dick McTaggart, as Olympic lightweight champion, but it was another 12 years before Britain tasted victory again, when Chris Finnegan lifted Gold at the 1968 Games in Mexico. Mixed fortunes followed for Terry. He was the toast of the East End and was photographed with the Kray Twins – ex-boxers themselves and huge fans of the fight game. Spinks played down the gangland association. 'I was popular, they were popular and they wanted to be seen with me, there was nothing more than that to it.' But though Terry's link with crime amounted to no more than a handshake and a photo, many feel that the publicity did him no favours. His cousin Rosemary ran a long campaign to win an MBE for the ex-boxer. While Finnegan and McTaggart were honoured, Terry was left aside.

'Family and friends have racked their brains trying to come up with an explanation,' says Rosemary. 'I once thought the fact Terry had been photographed with the Kray twins may have gone against him. Terry has never been in trouble in his life and I think it is disgraceful how he's been treated.' Fellow hero Finnegan added his weight to the campaign, saying: 'I was awarded the MBE only a few months after I'd won my gold. It is diabolical that Terry was left out.' Finally, the wrong was righted, Terry receiving the MBE in the 2002 New Year's Honours List.

> "Being snapped with fight fans the Krays did him no favours"

Terry never became bitter, though he took some hard punches in life. Two marriages collapsed as the boxer turned publican developed serious drink problems, and in 1994 he was taken into hospital. Alcohol was killing him, and cousin Rosemary decided to take care of him. The East End of London has since seen boxing gold again, most notably with Lennox Lewis and Audley Harrison. But neither could quite win hearts as well as bouts like the baby-faced Spinks.

Gentlemen, players and pugilists

The first Aussie cricket tour

The Australians are arguably the best cricket team in the world, feted, well looked after and travelling everywhere first class. But a century and a half ago it was very different.. The first Aussie tourists were Australian Aborigines. Before the tour was over one of them would be dead – a victim of the unfamiliar London weather – and buried in Bethnal Green. Unsung at Lords or the Gabba, he is remembered by a single eucalyptus tree planted in Meath Gardens.

When the cricketers disembarked at Gravesend on 13 May 1868 it was after a gruelling three-month voyage from Sydney. They even had to be smuggled out of Australia. When it became public that a group of white businessmen was planning on taking an Aboriginal team to England, the Victoria government did everything it could to stop it. Members warned the long trip, cold weather and the likely exposure to alcohol could have disastrous consequences for the players.

Reaction in England was mixed. *The Times* sniffily described the tourists as 'a travestie upon cricketing at Lord's', and described the men as 'the conquered natives of a convict colony'. *The Daily Telegraph* didn't think much of Australia. 'Nothing of interest comes from there except gold nuggets and black cricketers,' it declared. But the Aussies' skill and athleticism won many admirers, as they criss-crossed England in their frantic itinerary, playing 47 matches and taking the field for 99 days of a

King Cole and the Aussie Cricketers

possible 126. 'They throw in very well indeed, making the ball whizz along at a great pace,' reported the *Sporting Gazette*. The *Sheffield Telegraph* called the tour 'the event of the century', and *Reynolds News* described the games as marking 'a new epoch in the history of cricket'.

The team came from Edenhope in western Victoria, and owed their successes to sharp hand-eye co-ordination that put their white opponents to shame – the fielding and bowling particularly caught the eye of the fans. They wore white flannels and red shirts, and blue caps, each with a boomerang and cricket bat motif above the peak. And as a concession to a sheltered Anglo-Saxon audience (who believed they would be unable to tell black faces apart) each player had to wear a different-coloured sash.

There was more. The English fans wouldn't even attempt to get to grips with the players' aboriginal names, so they were given childlike nicknames to make it easy for the crowd. Bullchanach became Bullocky; Jumgumjenanuke Dick-a-Dick; Brimbunyah Redcap and so on. And Bripumyarrimin, soon to succumb to tuberculosis, was re-dubbed King Cole.

> "They were given new names to make it easy for fans"

The 11 played against the MCC at Lord's on 12 and 13 June, 1868. MCC batted first with Aussie all-rounder Johnny Mullagh taking 5-82 off 45 overs. He bowled the Earl of Coventry, knocking out his off stump. He took the top England scorer, Richard Fitzgerald, who made 50. The MCC amassed 164 and the Australians outbatted them with a first innings total of 185: Johnny Mullagh getting 75 and Lawrence 25. The English press could no longer mock the visitors.

Sadly it was to be King Cole's last match. Much weakened by his disease he died at Guy's Hospital on 24 June, 1868 ... just 11 days after the Test ended. He was buried in Victoria Park Cemetery, later to become Meath Gardens.

Gentlemen, players and pugilists

A team built of iron and steel

A century ago, a wealthy East End shipbuilder made an investment in a new sports ground for his works' football team. For Arnold Hills, it was another gambit in his long campaign to keep his workers away from the bottle and engage them instead in healthy outdoor pursuits. For the team, it was the first step that would take them to world fame and cup-winning glory.

When Hills' father Frank Hills bought the Thames Ironworks and Shipbuilding Company in 1880, he took on a going concern – but one with a decidedly mixed pedigree. The technology of iron and steel building was one of the new marvels of the science-obsessed 19th Century, and engineers everywhere were pushing back the boundaries. Thames Ironworks was at the forefront, building the Warrior, the world's first iron warship, at its Orchard Road works in Blackwall in 1859.

But the launch of another battleship, the Albion, was less happy. Launches regularly drew huge crowds and the company constructed a vast grandstand to hold the throng. The Ironworks' engineering skills let it down, literally, as the grandstand collapsed killing 200 people. The company's reputation was shot and, in 1880, the Hills family took over an ailing giant. It was always an uphill struggle. Arnold Hills was determined to keep his 6,000 men in jobs and maintained the yard at Blackwall when a move downstream to Tilbury would have made more econom-

West Ham United

ic sense. The Thames industry was under increasing attack from bigger firms on the Clyde, Tyne and Mersey. But Hills was no mere money man. Like many Victorian businessmen, he was a patrician with his workers' welfare at heart. He lived among them, in East India Dock Road and, after his short walk home, would spend evenings dreaming up schemes for their education and moral well-being.

The vegetarian Christian encouraged all his men to 'sign the pledge', to renounce the booze, but he knew that wasn't enough. He had to give them a counter-attraction to keep them out of the pubs. So in 1895, he founded Thames Ironworks Football Team.

The Football League had recently been founded and the game was quickly becoming a huge working-class sport. The team quickly took off – so much so that in 1897 Hills paid for a new stadium at the Memorial Ground, which boasted a grandstand and hosted athletics and cycling meets as well as soccer.

The shipyard was in trouble, and in 1911, the Ironworks built the Thunderer, the last ship ever to be constructed on the capital's great waterway. But as the Ironworks foundered, its offspring team

> "As the shipyard foundered the team grew in strength"

went from strength to strength. In 1900, the team were elected to the Southern League and became a Limited Company in their own right, severing their links with Thames Ironworks. And in 1904, under the new name of West Ham United, they moved to their present home in Upton Park.

Hills died in 1927. His legacy to the people of Blackwall wasn't the one he planned. His ironworks couldn't keep them in jobs but he gave them their own football club to cheer. The club's engineering roots are remembered in the crossed hammers on their crest. And that is why to this day you hear the crowds at Upton Park chanting 'Come on you Irons', a chant that dates back to shipbuilding days.

Gentlemen, players and pugilists

Whitechapel globetrotter

Basketball is, today, one of the world's most popular sports and Shaquille O'Neal is a household name. But 70 years ago the game was very different. It was American, it was small time – and it was white. One big reason basketball evolved into the billion-dollar business of today was a young Jewish lad from Whitechapel with a big cigar and bigger ideas.

Abe Saperstein's parents left Whitechapel in the early 1900s looking for a new life and fortune in the New World, taking their four-year-old boy with them. But it was Abe who was to make the fortune. In 1927 the young Saperstein was 24 years old and living in Chicago when he noticed the opportunity he'd been waiting for. In those days, black players weren't allowed in the professional basketball leagues, they had to play in separate 'junior' leagues. When Abe's local black team, the Savoy Big Five, broke up, he took them over.

Abe's idea was that the team wouldn't play the small leagues, with their limited market, but go out on the road, play one-off exhibition matches followed by a challenge match against a local amateur white team. It was a winning formula – each match was a novelty that would pull big crowds, and the black-white clash added an extra edge in the often segregated American towns. The Harlem Globetrotters were on their way.

Of course they weren't from Harlem, but that was the black centre of New York, and added to the image. The band travelled in a Stars and Stripes painted bus, they adopted the theme song *Sweet Georgia Brown* and, playing exhibition matches between their own two teams, they had plenty of opportunity to develop their jokey style and trick shots. The last part of the mix was a happy accident. During a game a player managed to set his vest on fire and, grabbing a bucket of water, he put it out. The crowd loved it, and Abe ensured clowning was worked into the act.

By the 1960s the Globetrotters were literally that and were hugely popular all over the world. They went on to have two audiences with the Pope and visited the White House to be made 'Ambassadors of Goodwill' by President Ford.

The Globetrotters were huge in Britain, filling Wembley again and again. And before his death in 1966, Abe returned to his native Whitechapel and, ever the showman, was photographed leaning on a Rolls-Royce, puffing on his trademark Havana.

> "He went back to Whitechapel and posed, leaning on a Rolls-Royce and puffing on a Havana"

The monster he created rolled on without him – 250 shows a year at its peak, but the game had changed. By the late 1970s the pro leagues, no longer segregated, were matching the traditional American sports of football and baseball in popularity. TV made the teams world famous and the biggest stars were black.

The Globetrotters had become a novelty act and no longer lured the best players. All the tricks they had pioneered were being outdone in the regular leagues, where stars like O'Neal, Chris Webber and Allan Houston command around $20m a season. The Globetrotters last visited London in 1991. It was a fitting tribute to Abe that their last game should be in the East End, as they said goodbye to English basketball at the London Arena, on the Isle of Dogs. Saperstein is buried in Westlawn Cemetery, Chicago.

Gentlemen, players and pugilists

Tough roots of Millwall FC

There can't be many more fervent hotbeds of football than the East End, and Tower Hamlets has certainly produced more than its fair share of soccer talent. Yet it's an irony that though the borough gave birth to two of the oldest football league teams, nowadays both play outside the area.

West Ham United have been gone for the best part of a century. Millwall, meanwhile, were still local lads until 1910, when they left the Isle of Dogs for a new home south of the river. But while they may have a reputation for hard-battling football on the pitch, it goes hand-in-hand with an unfortunate and only partly deserved reputation for crowd trouble off it – a reputation that has existed for almost as long as the club itself.

Like many of the early league teams, Millwall started off as a works side, giving the employees of JT Morton's jam and marmalade works a welcome dose of exercise. When the club was formed in 1885 the company's works, in West Ferry Road, on the Isle of Dogs, was still a new operation. Millwall Dock, at the southern end of the island, had only opened in 1864 – before that Millwall was a remote and unpopulated part of London.

But very soon the area was firmly industrial and populated with immigrant labour. Nearly all of the workers at Morton's were Scottish immigrants. In honour of their homeland they adopted the blue and white of the Scots flag as their team colours, and took the lion rampant of their country's flag as their symbol. The

Millwall FC

football club they set up was called Millwall Rovers. And the team had a ready-made fan base, in the thousands of men and boys who poured onto the island to work in the new docks. The uncompromising play of the Scots and the no-nonsense demands of the fans made Millwall a fearsome place to visit.

Things started badly though. The first ever fixture, on October 3, 1885, was against Fillebrook, from Leyton. Millwall lost 5-0. The side gradually improved, joining the old Southern League, and reaching the semi-finals of the FA Cup in 1903, losing 3-0 to Derby County in front of 45,000 fans at Villa Park.

Having gone through a name change to Millwall Athletic, they now became plain Millwall FC and played on the Isle of Dogs before moving to The Den at New Cross in 1910. The 1930s and 40s saw huge gates of 40,000 plus, and the noise of the crowd saw The Den became one of the most feared grounds in the country. Cold Blow Lane was closed on a number of occasions as violence spilled on to the pitch and streets around.

> "The first players and fans were tough Scottish dockers"

The decades since have seen the Lions yo-yoing up and down through the divisions, at one point becoming founder members of the old Fourth (now Third Division) by virtue of a relegation! George Graham took over in 1982, and handed a debut to the young Teddy Sheringham, still playing today for West Ham. Graham guided the club back up to the Second Division, before leaving for Arsenal. John Docherty led Millwall to the Second Division championship in 1988 and First Division football for the first time in the club's history. Sheringham and Tony Cascarino scored the goals that put Millwall top of the league, with a 3-2 win over QPR at The Den on 1 October, 1988. 2004 saw a first FA Cup Final against Manchester United and UEFA Cup football. In the 2006-07 season they will be playing in League One (the third tier of English professional soccer).

Gentlemen, players and pugilists

Doggett's Coat and Badge

It's the oldest continuing sporting contest in the world, but the running of Doggett's Coat and Badge Race on the Thames highlights one of the sadder aspects of the decline of The Thames as a port – the disappearance of the river traffic that once made the river as crowded as London's streets.

It's not just the big ships that have gone; there was once an armada of small boats that carried goods and people on the Thames. Today, the watermen and lightermen live on as the crews of the small boats that operate on the river, but once they were thousands strong. Their power rested on the fact that, for most of its history, the Thames only had one bridge. Until the mid-1700s, you either used London Bridge or used a boat and the watermen – the waterborne minicab drivers of their day – were happy for it to stay that way.

Unfortunately, like some of the unlicensed cab drivers today, there were rogue elements. Parliament passed Acts in 1514 and 1555 to regulate charges and stop the passengers being ripped off, but there were worse dangers than that. In 1566 a new Act formed the Company of Watermen, to put an end to 'divers and many misfortunes and mischances [caused by] evil and ignorant persons who robbed and spoiled of their [passengers'] goods ... and also drowned them'. So started the first City company formed not to protect its members but to protect the public *from* its members.

But in many other ways the company was just like its City

Doggett's Coat and Badge

Livery counterparts. There were strict limits on membership. Entry to the company was only granted after a seven-year apprenticeship, and you weren't likely to win that unless your dad or uncle was a waterman. From 1696 boats had to bear a licence and number and operate from an approved plying place, and tables of fares soon appeared.

In 1715, Thomas Doggett set up the famous race, a test of stamina and skill for young watermen who had just finished their apprenticeships. But just as it became an organised, regulated and very lucrative trade, it was already beginning to die. There were two reasons: the growth of London as the world's biggest port and the relaxation on bridge building over the Thames. People could now walk or take a steam ferry over the river. But as the watermen declined the lightermen flourished. The lighters unloaded cargoes from ships (making them 'lighter') and carried them into port. Watermen and lightermen now handled goods rather than human cargo.

Until recently, the men worked 16-hour shifts of hard and physically demanding work. Lighters (which were big empty hulks, all hold and not much else) might be towed into port by steam tugs. But for 'short' distances they would be driven by the crew. This driving consisted of two men, one on each side of the bow, rowing the boat in using huge, 26ft oars.

> "The men would drive the boats in by hand using huge, 26ft oars"

In the early fifties there were 6000 craft on the river, supported by 350 tugs, but by the late sixties the trade was dying. The closure of the up-river docks, and the birth of new container terminals at Tilbury saw the end of the business. The lightermen live on as the masters of the waste disposal vessels and dredgers you see on the Thames today. And once a year you can see a glorious glimpse of the past, as young Freemen of the Company contest Doggett's Coat and Badge Race.

Gentlemen, players and pugilists

When Jack put the gloves on

In the mid-1700s boxing was a brutal sport. Rules were few, bouts open-ended, and physical protection non-existent. The winner was the last man standing and the loser often paid with serious physical or mental damage... or even death.

This was a problem for Jack Broughton. Jack, the third heavyweight boxing champion of all England, augmented his waterman's wages with bare-knuckle street fighting, but increasingly trained and managed a stable of fighters. Modern boxers talk about leaving the fight in the gym due to over-training; Broughton's boys often couldn't make the fight at all because they had beaten one another so badly in the gym.

But rigorous training was needed to produce a bare-knuckle fighter capable of going dozens of rounds, so Jack set to thinking. His solution was to invent mufflers, the earliest boxing gloves, which made their first appearance in his Hanway Street gym in 1743. And Jack, having invested time and money in training promising young fighters and crowd favourites, saw the problem in their careers being curtailed by injury and death in the brutal prize fights so, at the same time, he devised his own set of competition rules.

The London Prize Ring rules were boxing's first, and pre-dated the more famous Queensbury Rules by a century or so. It would be a mistake to think that Jack had gone soft – in a handbill published during the 1740s, he described boxing as simply the most

Jack Broughton

successful method of beating a man deaf, dumb, lame and blind. But his ideas proved so effective in prolonging the careers of fighters that the rules he prepared in 1743 remained in effect until 1838. In their new form, they were the benchmark for fighting until the last bare-knuckle championship bout in 1889. After 1889, gloves became the rule, so Broughton's ideas persist to this day in the fight game.

The rules were as follows: no hitting below the belt; no hitting an opponent who was down; wrestling only allowed above the waist; fights to be contested in rounds, with a 30-second rest period in between; rounds to be over with a knockdown; and fights over after a rest period if a fighter couldn't toe the mark or come up to scratch (sayings that entered the language). This mark was a square of a yard chalked in the middle of a stage which boxers had to approach at the start of each new round.

The rules were sponsored by Jack's patron, William Augustus, the Third Duke of Cumberland. Augustus was to become known as Butcher Cumberland for his merciless slaughter of Jacobite Scots at the Battle of Culloden in 1745. The Duke also had a taste for bloody sports, wagering huge amounts on Jack's successful fights.

> "Boxers were training so fiercely that they were done before the fight"

As a sideline, Jack began to teach sparring with mufflers to the young relatives of the Duke of Cumberland. But the pair fell out big time after Broughton was beaten by Jack Slack in 1750. Cumberland lost £10,000 on the fight, and he lost his interest in pugilism soon afterwards. He may have fallen from favour with Cumberland. His erstwhile sponsor (voted the 18th century's Worst Briton in 2005 by *BBC History Magazine*) died at 45, his military career in shreds. Jack, meanwhile, enjoyed a long and comfortable retirement. He died in 1789, a wealthy 85 year old, still a national hero, and was buried in Westminster Abbey.

Gentlemen, players and pugilists

Ring masters of the East End

When Lennox Lewis landed the world heavyweight title in 1992, it ended a near-century wait for a British champion. But why so long? Once, the East End alone was churning out champs. There are some who challenged Lewis's cockney credentials though (more Canada than Canning Town). That had happened with the last undisputed English champion of the world too. Bob Fitzimmons, who held the title in 1897, may have been born in Cornwall, but was raised in New Zealand, did his early fighting in Australia and was twice crowned as an American world champion.

Lennox was born and raised in Stratford and professes a lifelong allegiance to West Ham United. Although his accent owes a little more to North America than east London, his career as a winning fighter puts him in a great East End tradition – of cockney kids using the ring to make their fame, if not their fortune. Go to Paradise Row in Bethnal Green and you'll see a blue plaque to the memory of Daniel Mendoza. Mendoza the Jew, as he was known, an ancestor of Peter Sellers, was English bareknuckle boxing champion from 1794 to 1795. With bouts lasting until one of the contenders dropped – often several hours – long reigns as champ weren't common.

The East End doesn't breed too many boxers the size of Mike Tyson, Evander Holyfield or even Mendoza – it's at the lighter weights that most of our lads have won their world crowns.

The East End Boxers

Gershon Mendeloff was born in Whitechapel on 24 October 1894, but it was as Ted 'Kid' Lewis that he held the world welterweight title between 1915 and 1916. Lewis fought an extraordinary 279 bouts in a career stretching from 1909 to 1929. Lewis was a graduate of Premierland, a boxing hall just off the Commercial Road. This Aldgate hall was the training ground of another two world champions. Teddy Baldock was a Premierland bantamweight, who in 1927 beat Archie Bell in London to claim the vacant British and World titles.

The third graduate was another Jewish East Ender, Jack 'Kid' Berg, the Whitechapel Whirlwind. Berg wasn't considered much of a contender when he burst onto the American fight scene on 31 May 1928. The little fighter, born Judah Bergman, was considered cannon fodder for Pedro Amador's junior welterweight world title bout.

But instead of the upright stance, limited movement and china chin of the classic British fighter, the Yanks were shocked as the whirling dervish – his range and angle of delivery of punches making him impossible to fight – put Amador on the canvas.

"Berg rocked the Yanks, expecting English cannon fodder"

Berg ripped through the division, fighting weekly, only failing when he tried to step up to the more moneyed lightweight crown, against Billy Petrolle. But though he took a beating against Petrolle, he fought on for another decade and died at the ripe old age of 82 in 1991.

View Charlie Magri's birth certificate and you see 20 July, 1956, Tunis. But Magri was Bethnal Green through and through, honing his speed and skills as a flyweight at numerous York Hall bouts from 1977 onwards. By 1979 he was European champ and four years later landed the WBC world crown, defeating Eleoncio Mercedes in London. Perhaps the saving of the legendary York Hall is a good omen – the East End could use another champion.

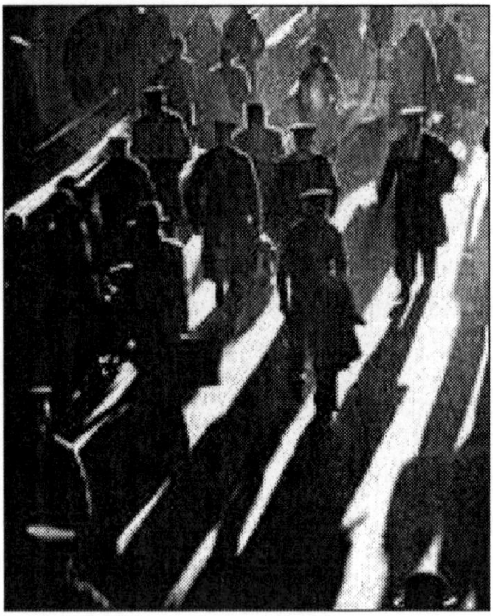

Preachers, priests and visionaries

John Wesley 124, Fred Charrington 126, Emmanuel Swedenborg 128, John Newton 130.

The father of Methodism

John Wesley was born in Lincolnshire, studied at Oxford University, served as a Church of England minister and worked as a missionary in America. But it was a religious experience in the East End of London that fired his faith and caused one of the greatest splits in the Church of England since the Middle Ages.

John was born in 1703, the son of rector Samuel. Wesley Snr was a devout, scholarly high churchman but it was a more dramatic childhood incident that marked the young John for life. At the age of six, he was rescued by a neighbour from a burning room in the rectory. The narrow escape left a deep scar and gave him a belief that he had been spared for a purpose – and for the rest of his days, he flung himself tirelessly into fulfiling it.

At Oxford, Wesley's piety came to the fore as he and his brother, Charles, led a group of students nicknamed 'The Holy Club', which would meet for Bible study, prayer and discussion. Soon their methodical approach earned them a new name: 'The Methodists'. By 1735 the two brothers were ordained Anglican priests but, rather than following their father into a comfortable country parsonage, they decided to spread that they would spread the word to the New World.

On the journey, the pair encountered a group called the Moravians who had a simple faith in Christ, a strong emphasis on the death of Jesus and a powerful missionary zeal. Their faith

John Wesley

opened John's eyes. During a violent storm on the journey, when he thought that he would die, he was amazed at the attitude of the Moravians who simply prayed and showed no fear. In 1738 the pair returned to England. The Moravians had shaken the foundations of Wesley's Anglican practices. And in May 1738, at a meeting in Aldersgate Street, a change was to come over him which would alter the course of the Church in England. Wesley had sat reading the words of Martin Luther. He records what happened next in his journal.

'He was describing the change which God works through faith in Christ. I felt strangely warmed. I felt I did trust in Christ alone for salvation and an assurance was given me that he had taken away my sins and saved me from the laws of sin and death.' It was a turning point for the Wesleys' ministry. John preached his new vision at Spitalfields, St John at Wapping, St Paul's, Shadwell, and St Matthew's in Bethnal Green.

The evangelising minister travelled, on horseback or coach, a quarter of a million miles, preaching 40,000 times. On his travels, he became painfully aware of the lot of the poor, and how little their local priests were doing for them.

> "He was appalled by conditions in Bethnal Green, worse than Newgate"

He described his horror at the scenes in Bethnal Green. 'There is such poverty as few can conceive without seeing it. I have not found such distress ... even in the prison of Newgate.'

Wesley drew huge crowds but he wasn't universally loved. He was banned from many Church of England pulpits, physically assaulted and constantly criticised. Wesley always wanted to remain in the Anglican Church. But soon after he died in 1793, the Methodists were forced out, causing a huge schism. By then, Methodism had 77,000 members in England and 470 preaching houses, numbers which have now grown to 20 million members in 62 countries.

Preachers, Priests and Visionaries

The pious brewer's boy

Frederick Charrington had everything going for him. He was young, tall, good-looking and, best of all, he stood to come into millions as heir to one of the great brewing families of the East End. But Fred was no idle son of the rich, he had a conscience and it was this that would change the course of his life dramatically.

Charrington was born in the East End, baptised at St Dunstan's, Stepney and raised in 3 Tredegar Place, later re-numbered 87 Bow Road. He was sent to the posh Marlborough public school but returned to the family home in the East End and it was here, as a young man, that the extraordinary coincidence occurred that would lead Fred to renounce his millions and work for the poor.

Passing the Rising Sun pub in Cambridge Heath Road, Bethnal Green, Charrington saw a sight within that was all too common in the Victorian East End. A woman with her three children in tow begged her husband for money, the drunken spouse hit his wife and Fred, unable to ignore any injustice, rushed in to pull the man off. He paused in horror. There, above the door was the name of the pub's proprietors .... Charrington.

He renounced the family millions and dedicated his life to helping the fallen and the falling and to fighting the 'evils' that dragged them down – alcohol, poverty and prostitution. Charrington would parade up and down outside the East End gin palaces, wearing a sandwich board which carried the dire warn-

Frederick Charrington

ing 'The wages of sin is death'. He kept watch on the numerous brothels, noting down the comings and goings in his little black book, handing details to the constabulary.

Needless to say, Fred's public spiritedness was not always welcome and he received many batterings from the prostitutes' pimps. And on one unfortunate occasion, the madame of an East End brothel was so distracted by the news that Charrington was approaching with his little black book that she rushed inside her house, had a heart attack and promptly died.

On Sundays Fred would lead his temperance brass band through Stepney and Wapping, stopping to tempt converts at the many pubs along the way – many of them bearing that name Charrington above their door. The throng would grow along the way, and by the end would contain a large number of good-natured and noisy drunks, who found 'Uncle Fred's' regular weekend procession very entertaining sport.

Many mocked Charrington, and his opposition to music halls made him appear as one of those grim Victorian philanthropists for whom any entertainment was morally suspect. But he left his monument and one that did immense good for generations of East Enders. Charrington, having renounced riches, campaigned vigorously to raise cash and build the Great Assembly Hall in Mile End Road. The mission, opened in 1886, fed the poor bodies with bread and cocoa and their souls with evangelistic religion. Before the phrase was ever coined, the mission was a centre of social work and, in 1910, provided Christmas dinner for 850 families.

Frederick Charrington died in 1936, one of the last of the great Victorian philanthropists. And just a few years later his mission would be gone too – burned down in the fires of the Blitz. Mile End's Charrington brewery shut down in 1975.

> "On Sundays Fred led his temperance band through East End streets"

Preachers, Priests and Visionaries

Visions in Wapping

Emanuel Swedenborg was born in Stockholm on 29 January 1688. The son of a clergyman, he grew up in a home filled with intellectual, philosophical, political and moral debate. He was certainly an intense child, writing later: 'From my fourth to my tenth year, I was constantly engaged in thought upon God, salvation, and the spiritual sufferings of men.'

Leaving Uppsala University at 22, he decided to travel Europe and immersed himself in an astonishing variety of disciplines: physics, astronomy, metallurgy, mineralogy, geology, chemistry, watchmaking, bookbinding and lens grinding. And the tireless Swedenborg was a creator too. He designed a submarine, an aeroplane, a steam engine, an air gun and a slow combustion stove.

From the 1720s, Swedenborg was dividing his time between Sweden and London. The English capital attracted him, because its free press allowed him to publish his often controversial works without hindrance or censorship. Arriving in Wapping, Swedenborg first made his home in Wellclose Square, near the Highway. Wellclose and Prince's Squares were lined with townhouses, built by the wealthy Swedish merchants who had settled in the area. These timber traders had wharves at Wapping, and soon the local Swedish community grew, with shopkeepers, craftsmen and itinerant sailors. In 1728, the community raised money for their own place of worship – and London's first Swedish church was built in Prince's Square.

Emmanuel Swedenborg

Swedenborg became a regular worshipper at the new church. He was still commuting between his native and adopted countries - returning to the Swedish parliament to deliver a paper on the future of the national currency, coming back to London to publish his groundbreaking works on the brain and cerebral cortex – but soon his life was to take an extraordinary turn.

In 1744 Swedenborg began to have vivid, disturbing and exhilarating dreams and visions. He told no-one, merely logging his experiences in his diaries. But trying to make sense of it all, he began a meticulous study of the Bible. Then, in April 1745, God appeared to him, telling him that he would reveal truths to humanity through Swedenborg.

Swedenborg published enormous amounts, expounding on the hidden, inner meanings of the stories of the Bible, and the fundamental nature of God, Humanity and Creation. He kept as low a profile as such a productive writer was able to. He published his work anonymously in London (his followers in Sweden were persecuted by the authorities), and he made no attempts to set up a church to disseminate his ideas.

On 29 March 1772, Swedenborg died at his Wapping home, and was buried in the little Swedish church in Prince's Square. Not much remains to be seen now. The Swedish community has long since dispersed, and the visionary's remains were removed to Uppsala Cathedral in 1908. The church closed in 1910 and, despite a fierce campaign, was demolished in 1921. In 1938, Prince's Square was renamed Swedenborg Square. But though the fine old houses of Swedenborg and Wellclose Squares escaped the Blitz, they couldn't dodge the planners. In the 1960s both were demolished as slums by the GLC.

> **"His life changed the night God paid him a personal visit. He claimed insight into the secrets of Creation"**

Preachers, Priests and Visionaries

Amazing grace saved Newton

John Newton crossed the seas of the world many times in his career as merchant seaman and slave trader. But none of his journeys was so great as that he made from a foul-mouthed dealer in human flesh to a humble minister of God.

Newton was born in Wapping on 24 July, 1725. He had a promising start. His father was commander of a merchant ship which sailed the Mediterranean, his mother a devout Christian who taught John at home, hoping that one day he would enter the ministry. But his mother died when he was just seven years old and, at the age of 11, John was at sea himself. He made six voyages with his father before the elder Newton retired.

In 1744, the hardened seaman was press-ganged onto a man-of-war, HMS Harwich. Even his father's friendship with the admiral couldn't get John released – England was about to go to war with France. Instead he got his son promoted, knowing an officer would have a better chance of surviving the voyage. But John found conditions intolerable and jumped ship at Plymouth. The unlucky Newton was quickly recaptured, publicly flogged and demoted from midshipman to common seaman. The crew was banned from showing him any kindness or even talking to him.

Finally at his own request he was exchanged into service on a slave ship, which took him to the coast of Sierra Leone. But if he thought life would be better out of the Navy, he was wrong. He became the servant of a slave trader and was brutally abused.

John Newton

Falling ill, he was ridiculed by his master's wife. And when he complained, his returning master chained him on deck, day and night, rain and scorching sun, with a pint of rice for his daily meal. Early in 1748 he was rescued by a sea captain who had known John's father. Newton worked his way up to become captain of his own ship – trafficking in slaves. The early religious instruction from his mother was now a distant memory. Newton was a coarsened, foul-mouthed character by now.

But while attempting to steer the ship through a storm, he had his 'great deliverance'. When all seemed lost and the ship would surely sink, he exclaimed, 'Lord, have mercy upon us.' He reflected that it was the first time in years that he had called on his Maker. In his cabin he reflected on what he had said and began to believe God had addressed him through the storm and that 'grace' had begun to work for him. For the rest of his life he saw May 10, 1748 as the day of his conversion, a day in which he abandoned his will to a higher power.

> "For the rest of his life he saw that day as a divine message"

In 1750 he married Mary Catlett, and by 1755 gave up seafaring. Now Newton met John Wesley, founder of Methodism. Inspired, he decided to become a minister and accepted the curacy of Olney, Buckinghamshire. Newton's church became so crowded during services that it had to be enlarged. One of the draws were the hymns he composed with his friend, the poet William Cowper ... among them *Amazing Grace*, *Glorious Things of Thee are Spoken* and *Come My Soul, Thy Suit Prepare*. He became Rector of St Mary Woolnoth, in the City, staying till his death in 1807. And Newton left another legacy. MP William Wilberforce, who was in agonies over whether to stay in politics or not, arranged a meeting with Newton to talk things through. Newton persuaded him to stay in politics, and Wilberforce would become the driving force behind the abolition of slavery.

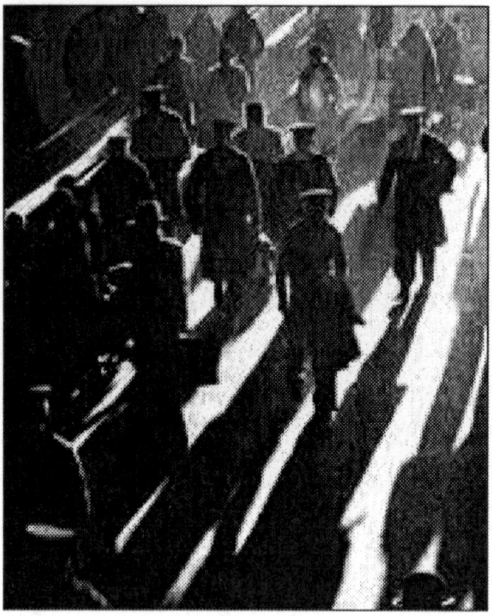

Musicians, composers and pop stars

Steve Marriott 134, Ronnie Scott 136, Peter Prelleur 138, Peter Green 140, Helen Shapiro 142, Wolf Mankewitz 144, Peter Grant 146, Billy Ocean 148, Jah Wobble 150.

Sad finale for the ace Face

In the early hours of 20 April, 1991 the people of the pretty Essex village of Arkesden were woken by flames. The firefighters fought their way through the charred wreckage of the thatched cottage but it was too late for the occupant. As Essex firefighter Keith Dunatis told the papers the next day, 'As soon as we found him we knew it was Steve Marriott. We all felt sad, we had been fans.'

Thirty years before the Britpop of Oasis and Blur, East End mod band the Small Faces had been the biggest thing in British pop music. Lead singer Steve Marriott was born in Stepney in 1947 and he grew up listening to music. 'My dad was a pub pianist, which meant he got his drinks free, which was the point. Everybody was singing, everybody was drunk and everyone was happy.' Music was in his blood and the young Steve started to earn cash by busking around the bus queues of Stepney with his ukelele. But mum had bigger things in mind and put him forward for auditions in the stage musical *Oliver!*, penned by another musical cockney, Lionel Bart. Steve wasn't keen but auditioned with a skiffle version of the Buddy Holly hit *Oh Boy*. Bart recognised the 11-year-old from his routine at East End bus stops and he got the job.

Just a year later Steve made his recording debut, on the *Oliver!* soundtrack album, singing lead vocals on *Consider Yourself*, *I'd Do Anything* and *Be Back Soon*. But despite a spell at the Italia

Steve Marriott

Conti stage school in Islington – 'I didn't really act, just played cockney kids, which I was anyway,' remembered Steve – his ambitions lay elsewhere. And it all fell into place when he bumped into Ronnie Lane in a music store in Manor Park.

Ronnie was a Plaistow boy in a band called the Outcasts, with drummer Kenney Jones, from Stepney. But the Outcasts were going nowhere and, with a shared interest in the music of James Brown, Smokey Robinson and Otis Redding, the trio knew they belonged together. And they had a name when a girlfriend of band member Jimmy Winston saw the three together and blurted out 'Cor, ain't you got small faces!' The final piece fitted when keyboard player Ian McLagan joined the band. Like the rest of the band, he was a tiny Londoner with a cheeky sense of humour. Like four Artful Dodgers (the oversized Winston had now been cast aside) the Small Faces set forth to conquer the charts.

> "They had fame but no money. Superstars on £20 a week"

Between 1965 and 1969 the band were rarely out of the charts with hits like *Sha La La La Lee*, *Itchycoo Park* and *All Or Nothing*. The only mod band who were mods themselves, Marriott believes their distinctive sound could only have come from the East End. 'We were a mix of R&B and music hall. The R&B came from Detroit the music hall from Stepney. That's what *Itchycoo Park* is about ... having a drink and a party.'

But the party had to end. Like many Sixties bands, the Small Faces didn't read the small print when they signed their contract and spent their career as megastars on £20 a week. Steve passed the Seventies and Eighties in pub bands, but that day in 1991 had just returned from recording a new album in LA with old pal Peter Frampton. It was going to put them back in the big time, but a jetlagged Marriott, befuddled by alcohol and valium, fell asleep with a cigarette burning – and the story of Stepney's Artful Dodger was over.

Musicians, Composers and Pop Stars

Five-bob sax the route to fame

Lester Young, Coleman Hawkins, Charlie Parker – it's not an unbreakable law, but to be a great of the jazz saxophone usually means you're black, American and probably from Chicago, Detroit or New York. Ronnie Scott was a white Jewish boy from Wapping. But it didn't stop him becoming one of the most influential saxophonists of his day, and the founder of a jazz institution that still bears his name

Memories of the East End stayed with Ronnie Scott (born Ronald Schatt) all his life. The stables on Cable Street, with a dairy next door where he would take a jug to fetch fresh milk from the cows. Trips to Petticoat Lane where he would listen to his grandmother haggle with the stallholders, and jellied eels from Tubby Isaacs stall afterwards. Reading, aeroplanes and football were passions for the schoolboy, now at Raines Foundation in Whitechapel Road, but soon his sights were set on America. Musicians like Coleman Hawkins and Lester Young were inventing a new kind of music. An inspired Ronnie bought an old cornet from an East End junk shop – but the five shilling instrument disintegrated almost immediately. Returning to the shop he picked up a soprano sax and was on his way.

Soon he was making a reputation for himself at Jewish youth club dances around the East End. And then he and his friends progressed to the West End. It was the late forties and the clubs were full of American GIs. Here Ronnie heard records by the likes of

Ronnie Scott

Tommy Dorsey, Duke Ellington and Artie Shaw, and memorised every note. In 1947, Ronnie, then 20, blew his savings on a trip to New York to see for himself what the jazz scene there was all about. It was 'a fantastic experience' he remembered later. He'd never heard an American group in a proper club atmosphere. On one memorable night Ronnie heard Charlie Parker play with Miles Davis at the Three Deuces. Playing next door was the Dizzy Gillespie Big Band and, late into the night, Davis sat in with Gillespie. Ronnie's dream was to set up a club in London.

The dream came true in October 1959, the day him and pal Pete King opened their club at 39 Gerrard Street, Soho. The best of British jazz played at the new club, but in November 1961 came a groundbreaking booking. America's Zoot Sims was booked in for a four-week residency, paving the way for guest appearances by US greats including Roland Kirk, Stan Getz, Ben Webster, Bill Evans, Wes Montgomery and many more. And the respect was mutual. Charles Mingus said in 1961: 'Of the white boys, Ronnie gets closest to the negro blues feeling.'

> "A musician who would take an old tune and give it new life"

By the 1990s Ronnie's health was beginning to suffer. A heavy smoker for many years, he suffered thrombosis, having two operations on his legs. Worse was to come. Teeth problems forced him to stop playing. A lengthy and painful course of teeth implants didn't help. After a year unable to play, the surgeons came to fit the new teeth and found the bone structure wasn't large enough – for a man who lived to play it was devastating.

Teetotal Ronnie began to drink, exacerbating his depression. Mixing brandy with sleeping pills was dangerous, and on 23 December 1996, Ronnie suddenly died, the verdict 'death by misadventure'. To his friends it was a huge shock, but Spike Milligan remembered the good times, and 'a magnificent jazz musician' who 'would take an old tune and give it new life'.

Musicians, Composers and Pop Stars

The forgotten composer

Peter Prelleur, organist, composer, tutor and author, is largely forgotten now, but he was one of the most important musical figures of the early 1700s. For although it might not be mentioned in the same breath as Salzburg, Paris or Hamburg, the East End had a thriving classical tradition in the early years of the 18th century, much of it centred on the celebrated churches of Nicholas Hawksmoor.

Prelleur led a curious musical double life. This East End Huguenot had anglicised his original Christian name of Pierre. He lived in Rose Lane, which has long since made way for Commercial Street. And in his day job he played the organ in Christ Church, Spitalfields and composed religious music.

This was one of the grandest positions in London; the organ, built for the church in 1735 by Richard Bridge, was the largest in Georgian England, with more than a thousand pipes. Even Handel had played on the Christ Church organ. Prelleur had also been the organist at St Alban's Church in Wood Street.

But in the evenings, Prelleur played to a quite different audience – in the Angel and Crown tavern in Whitechapel. An advertisement in the *London Daily Post* of August 21 1739 gives a flavour of those evening shows: 'Rope dancing, posture masters, singing and dancing, serious and comic. The whole to conclude with a new entertainment called *Harlequin Hermit* or *The Arabian Courtezan* ... with a complete band of music, consisting

Peter Prelleur

of kettle drums, trumpets, French horns, hautboys and violins. The music by an eminent master.' The master was Peter Prelleur of course. And the fact that he was as happy to play in a pub as he was in a church could be attributed to his enthusiasm for bringing music to as many people as possible. He was also the harpsichordist and composer for Goodman's Fields Theatre.

Prelleur had already composed his seminal work, a guide for musicians entitled *The Modern Musick-Master or The Universal Musician*. This seminal 1731 work contained 'an introduction to singing, after so easy a method, that persons of the meanest capacities may (in a short time) learn to sing (in tune) any song that is set to musick.'

It had 'directions for playing on the flute: with a scale for transposing any piece of musick to the properest keys for that instrument ... the newest method for learners on the german flute, as improv'd by the greatest masters of the age ... instructions upon the hautboy ... the art of playing on the violin ... the harpsichord illustrated and improv'd ... with a brief history of musick ... to which is added a musical dictionary ... Curiously adorn'd with cuts representing the manner of performing on every instrument.'

"Prelleur was a master of classical music yet he was as happy to play in a pub as in a church"

Prelleur, in fact, had written a complete guide to playing all the popular instruments of the day. A little translation is necessary for modern readers. The hautboy is the modern oboe. What Prelleur knew as the German flute is nowadays simply a flute, while (rather confusingly) what he called a flute is now the recorder. Peter Prelleur's mission, in church, in pubs and in his musical tutor, was to open up music to as many 18th century East Enders as possible. Little did he know that his *Modern Musick-Master* would still be instructing musicians 300 years later.

Lost genius of Fleetwood Mac

Fleetwood Mac continue to trundle around the stadiums of America, one of the world's biggest-selling bands still going strong after nearly 40 years. Meanwhile, the musical genius who started the band, and penned their earliest hits, may be settling down to practise the guitar, and reflecting on the millionaire lifestyle he rejected.

Fleetwood Mac founder Peter Green was born Peter Greenbaum in Bethnal Green in October, 1946. One day, one of his brothers bought home a cheap Spanish guitar and – when he tired of it – it was passed on to ten-year-old Peter. 'My brother showed me a few chords and I took off,' he remembered. His influences were varied – the twanging style of Hank Marvin from the Shadows and some old Jewish songs he learned from his family. But it was the American blues of Muddy Waters and BB King which would have a lasting influence, and turn him into one of the greatest rock guitarists of the Sixties.

Peter played bass in a variety of East End amateur bands before joining Peter B's Looners, as lead guitarist, in 1966. There he met Mick Fleetwood, the drummer in Fleetwood Mac till this day.

His big break came just three months later when he joined John Mayall's Bluesbreakers. The band had been favourites for years in the top West End music clubs and such stars as Rod Stewart and Long John Baldry were former members. Peter's task was to fill the shoes of the departing lead guitarist – one Eric Clapton.

Peter Green

Mayall had already got a replacement but, as he recalled later: 'This cocky cockney kid kept coming down and saying: 'I'm much better than he is!' He was, so we gave him a go.' The graffiti round London at the time read 'Clapton is God' and the fans took a lot of winning over. But Green's melancholy voice and haunting blues guitar style got them hooked. He also fitted in well with the existing rhythm section of Mick Fleetwood and John McVie.

Just a year later, the trio were ready to go it alone but, though Green was the undoubted star, his shyness came to the fore with the choice of band name – Fleetwood Mac. They made their debut at the Windsor Jazz and Blues Festival in 1967 and just months later, in early 1968, were recording their first album. By now Green was not just a blues hero, he was a pop star too, writing huge hits like *Albatross* and *Black Magic Woman*. But even as he first tasted stardom, Green seemed unhappy, uncomfortable with the fame and fortune.

He began experimenting with LSD and became interested in religion, suggesting to the other band members that they keep the bare minimum of their earnings and give the rest to charity. The others were none too impressed. With Green seemingly losing his sanity, he left the band in 1970 and became a hermit, rarely seeing his old friends. McVie recalled: 'I prefer to remember him before he left. Seeing him upset me too much.'

As Fleetwood Mac became a supergroup in the 70s and 80s, with albums such as *Rumours* and *Tusk*, Green kept a low profile.But after years of silence, he is back on stage and is, to the relief of his old pals, recording. 'He's back in the studio,' said Fleetwood. 'He's actually playing again, which is why he's here on this planet. I do seriously believe he has a magic touch.'

> "He suggested the band give their royalties to charity. They weren't impressed"

Musicians, Composers and Pop Stars

Long walk back to happiness

Pop careers have always been fleeting and all too often the stars find themselves out of the limelight without a penny to show for their brief taste of fame. But there can't be too many people who find themselves labelled a has-been at 18, after many successful years in the music business.

East End girl Helen Shapiro was always a precocious talent. It was March 1961 when the 14-year-old schoolgirl went straight to the top of the charts with the appropriately titled *Don't Treat Me Like A Child*. It was the beginning of a crazy career that saw her topping the bill at the London Palladium before getting home to bed in time to be at her school desk the next morning. Most people couldn't believe that the astonishingly deep and full voice was that of a schoolgirl – indeed many disc jockeys thought that it was actually a man singing!

Helen, the daughter of a Jewish tailor, swiftly followed that hit with two Number One singles, including her best known song *Walking Back To Happiness*. It was probably inevitable that Helen's (first) career would be as short as it was. She occupied that brief period between the late-1950s invasion of the British charts by American rockers Elvis Presley, Gene Vincent, Eddie Cochrane and the rest, and the UK response of Beat Music in the early 1960s. It was a time when Billy Fury, Cliff Richard and Rory Storm ruled the charts. But most were swept away by the boom in guitar groups which lay just around the corner.

Helen Shapiro

Shapiro appeared on a bill with an unknown Mersey band called The Beatles in 1963 and could already see the writing on the wall. 'That was the point when I thought: "Uh oh, something is changing,"' recalls Helen. 'The novelty thing was wearing off. The thing that really did it was the whole idea of groups. The majority of demonstrative record buyers were girls, and they went for the fellas. The Beatles upsurge was down to them.'

The irony was that Helen was still younger than the teenagers who were taking her place and had grown up being inspired by just the same artists. 'When I was 10, Elvis Presley was the coming thing, followed by Buddy Holly and the Everly Brothers, then Paul Anka and Neil Sedaka,' she said. But Britain's initial answer to rock and roll was very different to Elvis' and Eddie Cochrane's take on Black R&B. Like Lennon and McCartney, Helen's first musical efforts were in the skiffle music taken into the charts by the likes of Lonnie Donegan. At the age of just 10, Helen and her brother Ron formed a band with another East End star of the future.

> "Nobody could believe this big voice came from a little girl"

'Our group included Marc Bolan, who was nine and lived down the road,' she remembered. 'He was called Mark Feld then and was very chubby and very into Cliff.' Helen's break came when she caught the attention of legendary Columbia A&R man Norrie Paramor, who had worked with The Shadows and Adam Faith. It started a fantastic, but brief, run of success for the East End girl. Like so many others, when it was over, she was left with nothing and in the Nineties embarked on a fight with EMI, still paying her a derisory farthing-per-record royalty.

Today, still only in her fifties, Helen is in the middle of a successful second career, releasing religious records and acting in theatre. 'I've come of age,' she laughs. 'I'm more contented and would never swap the life I have now for the pressures of my teens.' It has been a long, but satisfying, walk back to happiness.

Artist's eye and business brain

Antiques dealer, best-selling author, playwright, screenwriter and entrepreneur – Wolf Mankewitz, was a man of many parts. But his twin loves – of literature and turning a profit on a deal – were forged in his childhood memories of his dad selling books from a barrow in Brick Lane.

In the 1950s and 60s, Mankewitz would gain fame and fortune as the writer of the hit musical *Expresso Bongo*, the best-selling novel *Make Me An Offer* and the science fiction thriller movie *The Day The Earth Caught Fire*. But as a boy, money was always hard to come by. His parents were Russian Jews, just one couple out of the thousands of immigrants who poured into Whitechapel in the late 19th and early 20th century.

Like many others, his dad struggled to make a living. But what he did have was industry and the thing he knew well was books. And it was a book on his father's stall that persuaded a young Wolf where his destiny lay. He picked up a copy of Bunyan's *Pilgrim's Progress* and was hooked – he decided to be a writer. His parents were determined their son should get the chances they had not had. And when Wolf won a scholarship to Cambridge University his father sold all the stock from his barrow to pay his way.

The £90 allowed Wolf to take up his course. But seeing the sacrifices his parents had to make made him determined never to suffer such privations again. For the rest of his life he would combine the vocation of writer with a buying-and-selling dealer's brain that owed a lot to his father's example.

Graduating from Cambridge at the precociously early age of 19, his first move was to set himself up as an antiques dealer. It quickly made him a good living, especially as he could combine it with his love of writing. His expert knowledge of Wedgewood china allowed him to pen the book *Wedgewood*, an informed guide to judging and buying pieces. But as the 1950s drew on, Wolf was to find fame not as a dealer, but as a successful writer. The best authors always write about what they know, they say, and he next turned to a fictionalised account of the antiques trade.

The very title of *Make Me An Offer* paints a picture of the deal-making stall traders Mankewitz had been surrounded by as a boy, and it described the wrinkles, tricks and occasional dodgy dealings of the trade.

Many cinemagoers of the time will remember the movie of his hit story *A Kid For Two Farthings*, a poignant tale of a lad who is conned into buying a one-horned goat on the pretext that it is a unicorn. And *The Bespoke Overcoat* again drew on his roots, telling the tale of an East End Jewish tailor. Both the hit films starred another East End Jew, David Kossoff. Mankewitz found notoriety, too, disrupting 1960s satire programme *That Was The Week That Was* with a verbal attack on critic Bernard Levin, who had had the temerity to attack his work. Mankewitz hammered home his point by having a tiny coffin – tailormade for the diminutive critic – delivered to his *Daily Express* office.

"Espresso Bongo was a vibrant musical slice of 1950s London"

It was a colourful life – toward the end of it he somehow became the honorary Panamian Consul to Dublin. But as far as he travelled, his hallmark was the eye for a deal, a razor sharp eye developed at his street trader dad's barrow in the Whitechapel of the 1920s and 30s.

Musicians, Composers and Pop Stars

The man who made Zeppelin

From the Small Faces and Helen Shapiro, to enigmatic Fleetwood Mac guitar virtuoso Peter Green, The The main man Matt Johnson and bass guitar guru Jah Wobble, cockney talent has spanned five decades of pop music. But of all the larger than life figures emanating from Tower Hamlets none was larger, or more infamous, than the manager who made Led Zeppelin the biggest band on the planet – Peter Grant.

Born into a broken – and painfully poor – Bethnal Green home on 5 April 1935, Grant had to provide for himself from an early age. He left school at 14 to work in a sheet metal factory, swiftly moving on to become a runner for the newspapers on Fleet Street. It was the start of a series of colourful jobs.

After National Service in the Army, Grant returned to the East End, turning his enormous 250lb bulk to his advantage by fighting as a professional wrestler and appearing in a film as a double for king-size actor Robert Morley. It was the late 50s and dance halls were giving way to rock and roll. Grant began arranging concerts for visiting rockers such as Gene Vincent, the Everly Brothers and Chuck Berry, and honed his organisational skills as one of Britain's first real tour managers.

Until now, the bookers had sat in their London offices while the bands hiked up and down the A1 in tatty old vans. Grant broke the mould by travelling with them, making sure they arrived on

Peter Grant

time, arranging their itineraries and, vitally, ensuring that they got paid – getting ripped off by promoters was standard.

As the 1960s drew on, native talent was supplanting the American bands and Grant was placed to manage the up-and-coming talent. Working with top producer Mickie Most, Grant took the Animals to America, then came home to manage the Yardbirds and the New Vaudeville Band. By the late 60s, the hard-nosed cockney had the knowledge and contacts to create the first supergroup. Led Zeppelin started off as an unsuccessful spin-off, the tired dregs of the New Yardbirds. That they became big was as much down to Grant as their own musical excellence.

Grant's power and menace became legendary. At a time when most bands were managed by ex-public schoolboys like the Rolling Stones' Andrew Loog Oldham or the Yardbirds' Simon Napier-Bell, he brought a streetwise style honed in his tough teenage years in Bethnal Green. That style consisted of, first and last, looking after his lads. In an era when promoters took 90 per cent of the gate giving 10 per cent to the band, Grant reversed the odds, making Robert Plant, John Paul Jones, Jimmy Page and John Bonham and himself rich in the process.

> "Musicians had always been ripped off ... but that was about to change"

Bootleggers were his pet hate. He was often seen prowling outside gigs in the early seventies with a baseball bat, confiscating and destroying the wares of hapless merchandisers outside.

Grant's heart went out of the business when his pal John Bonham, the band's giant drummer, died in 1980. He decided it was time to retire. The man who was part manager, part accountant, part fixer, part father and part minder to Led Zeppelin retreated to his Sussex estate to look after his two children and his collection of classic cars. Peter Grand died there of a heart attack on 21 November, 1995.

Musicians, Composers and Pop Stars

Tailormade for chart success

Sam Wolman used to scoff when the young tailor's assistant came into his chemist shop on Brick Lane to buy throat sweets, talking about his dreams of making it big in the music business. 'That was when he was nothing,' remembers the proprietor of Wolman's with a laugh. 'The next thing I knew he was on *Top of the Pops*!' The young no-hoper was one Leslie Sebastian Charles, but he would become better known to fans of pop music and the movies as Billy Ocean.

Leslie was born on 21 January, 1950, in Trinidad. Like many other West Indian families in the Fifties, the Charleses emigrated to England in search of work, and their son became an East Ender. He had dreams of making it in the music business but had to find a day job while working on his performing career. That's how he ended up working in the Spitalfields rag trade. But all that changed forever when he scored a brace of hits on the GTO label as a solo artist. *Love Really Hurts Without You* charted in 1976 and *Red Light Spells Danger* followed it into the Top 10 in 1977. A successful career seemed to beckon but, like so often in the fickle world of the pop charts, the initial momentum of his career was hard to maintain.

Billy's subsequent releases struggled for radio play and, between 1980 and 1984, Ocean was absent from the UK charts. But, with the kind of determination that powers pop longevity, he turned his attention to a bigger target – the US charts. Ocean

Billy Ocean

decamped to America at the turn of the Eighties and had a string of successes in the US R&B chart. Then he broke into the mainstream US charts and the hits crossed the Atlantic to make it big in Britain too. *Caribbean Queen (No More Love On The Run)* was Ocean's first national US pop Number 1, and it swiftly became an enormous hit in Britain. He followed the million-selling 1984 single with *There'll Be Sad Songs (To Make You Cry)* in 1986 and *Get Outta My Dreams, Get Into My Car* two years after that. It was a dazzling period of chart success, with both records going to Number 1 in the United States as well as being huge hits over in Britain.

Suddenly continued the astonishing run of successes, but Billy hit his UK high point in 1986 with another Number 1 hit. *When The Going Gets Tough, The Tough Get Going* was the theme song to the smash-hit film *The Jewel Of The Nile*, starring Michael Douglas. The video featured Douglas and co-stars Kathleen Turner and Danny de Vito dancing with Ocean, with the quartet dressed in white tuxedos.

Chart success in the UK started to wane once more but Billy, with the canny business sense that had seen him kick-start his career in the States, was one step ahead. He had released *Caribbean Queen* in Africa as *African Queen* and on the Continent as *European Queen*, each with specially-rewritten lyrics tailored to its new market! Just like the old days in the Brick Lane tailors, he was cutting his material to fit. Both versions were just as successful as the original, and it was to the European dance market that the singer now turned his attentions. Today, Billy is a force on the European music scene, though *When The Going Gets Tough, The Tough Get Going* was covered by Boyzone and became a Number 1 in Britain for the second time around.

> "I used to laugh when he said he'd be a star. Next thing he was on Top of the Pops"

Musicians, Composers and Pop Stars

The fall and rise of Wobble

A few years before John Lydon (Johnny Rotten) and John Beverley (Sid Vicious) were rattling the Establishment as the Sex Pistols, they struck up a teenage friendship with a Stepney lad named John Wardle. It was to lead to some of the most interesting and esoteric music of the 1970s and beyond.

Wardle, despite by his own admission 'not getting on too well with education' found himself at Kingsway College in 1973 alongside the two future Pistols. In fact it was a drunken introduction from Beverley, mangling Wardle's name, that led Lydon to re-christen him 'Jah Wobble'. By late 1977, Lydon and Beverley were part of the most notorious band UK music had ever seen. But by 1978 the Sex Pistols had imploded. Lydon left the band amid the wreckage of a disastrous, drunken and drug-fuelled US tour and went in search of more musically satisfying ventures. He quickly hooked up again with his old friend Wobble, who was drawing on their mutual love for dub reggae to develop a bass guitar sound revolutionary in white rock music. Together with Martin Atkins and Keith Levene, they formed Public Image Ltd, which fused Lydon's vicious and bitter lyrics to music far more interesting than anything the Pistols had created.

'Nobody had listened to the bass guitar in white music before,' commented Lydon, and the rumbling melodic basslines Wobble created owed much more to reggae than rock. Again, his style owed a lot to his mistrust of formal education. He threw away his

Jah Wobble

bass instruction book, eschewed formal lessons and made it up as he went along. 'Miles and miles ahead' was how the *New Musical Express* described the sound at the time. 'Some of the most awesome and original basslines in modern music' wrote the Melody Maker. Yet amazingly he had only picked up a bass guitar (lent by Sid Vicious) a few months before joining the band.

But just as the Pistols had imploded so did PIL. In 1980, wracked by drink and drugs the band started to fall apart and Wobble left. His stock had quickly risen in the music business, and the early eighties saw him working as a session musician, making solo records and collaborating with everyone from U2's The Edge to Holger Czukay of German experimental rock group Can. Meanwhile, his solo albums were drawing on a bewildering range of influences. Asian and African sounds were now rubbing up against the rock and reggae notes in his playing.

But in the late eighties he simply vanished. Battling the booze and exhausted by the pressures of producing album after album and playing live, the workaholic Wobble threw it all up and went to work for London Underground. He rose quickly through the ranks, from sweeping stations, to driving tube trains, before emerging back above ground in the early nineties.

> "He threw away the instruction book and reinvented the bass"

The 1991 hit *Visions of You*, with wobbling bassline, and vocals shared with Sinead O'Connor announced his return, and over the following decade Wobble resumed the relentless workload. Now free from the bottle he worked from his Bethnal Green base with his new band The Invaders of the Heart. Collaborating with Bjork, The Orb, Massive Attack, Primal Scream, The Shamen and many more – Wobble added his distinctive rumbling and liquid bass. He likes to mix it all up, but then he's an odd mix himself. As he told the *NME* back in the seventies: 'I've always been confident in what I do, yet I've always had a fear of rejection.'

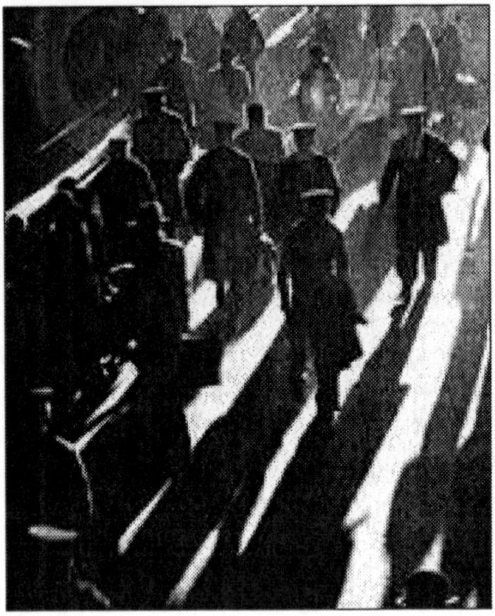

Inventors, architects and pioneers

IK and Marc Brunel 154, Joseph Bazalgette 156, Sir Hugh Platt, 158, John Dollond 160, Eugenius Birch 162, Benjamin Gompertz 164, John Rennie166, Robert Hooke 168, Nicholas Hawksmoor 170

Inventors, Architects and Pioneers

A bridge under the Thames

Today we take the Blackwall Tunnel for granted – confused lorry drivers excepted. But in the middle of the last century things were totally different. As London spread eastward, the north and south banks of the river found themselves isolated from each other. The Metropolitan Board of Works, the forerunner of the London County Council (which later became the GLC), wanted to get the lifeblood of the city, its people, moving to and from the booming new companies, with their desperate need for workers. So, in 1877, the Board paid £1.5 million to free the Thames bridges from tolls.

But the people living downstream of London Bridge received no benefit. Ferries were often halted due to the peasouper fogs. The problem became so bad that firms refused to employ staff who lived on the opposite banks.

People had been uniting the two banks of London with bridges since Roman times – it was the cheapest, safest and simplest way of building a crossing. But downriver there were problems caused by the twin demands of a wide span combined with the high clearance needed by the river's heavy traffic of ships. The answer was a new bridge and a tunnel. Tower Bridge was begun in 1888. And, with Shadwell too expensive a site for a new bridge, a tunnel was to be dug at Blackwall. There had been attempts before at tunnelling beneath the Thames – but the omens were not good. In 1798 a tunnel was started between Tilbury and

The Blackwall Tunnel

Gravesend, but was soon abandoned. The 1805 tunnel from Rotherhithe to Limehouse was more than 1,000ft long when it collapsed and was flooded.

In 1825, Isambard Kingdom Brunel started work on a masonry tunnel from Wapping to Rotherhithe using his new invention 'the shield' and Admiral Cochran's designs for tunnelling, which allowed miners to work in compressed air. The tunnel was designed for vehicles but was eventually opened as a foot tunnel in 1843. The public weren't keen and today it forms part of the Tube's East London Line. Then there was the Tower Subway. Built in 1869, it consisted of cast-iron segments and passengers were pulled through in a cable car. Later it briefly became a foot tunnel before closing 30 years later. It now carries water mains.

Undaunted, in 1887 Parliament passed the Blackwall Tunnel Act, allowing the building of two vehicle tunnels and a foot tunnel. All were designed by the Board of Works' chief engineer, Sir Joseph Bazelgette, a protege of Brunel. In 1888, though,

> "The omens for tunnels under the Thames were not good"

the new LCC settled on a larger vehicle tunnel, designed by Alexander Binnie. Pearson and Son won the tender, with a bid of £87,000, and in 1891 work began.

The technical demands were imposing. The tunnel would be bored by driving a shield through the soft earth, but the technology of the day did not allow curves in the cast-iron tunnel lining. The work was to be carried out in compressed air to hold back the water pressure. Many men had died in recent major engineering works and many had contracted 'the bends' from working in compressed air. But in 1897 the tunnel finally opened. A century later the 1,000 horse-drawn vehicles a day have been replaced by 35,000 motor vehicles (and a second tunnel). As Poplar councillor and later MP Will Crooks said of the tunnel: 'This great work will be remembered for all time.'

Inventors, Architects and Pioneers

The man who ended the stink

ONE thing we all take for granted today is clean, fresh water and plenty of it. But until just a century ago, East Enders were more likely to be killed by their water than revived by it. In the 1800s, as Tower Hamlets multiplied in size with the influx of immigrants from the countryside and abroad, cholera became a chronic threat to human health.

Look left out of the train window as you travel from Bromley-by-Bow to West Ham and you will see the distinctive rococo form of Abbey Mills pumping station. It may look like something from a horror film but, in its day, it made the East End a safe place to live and work, as it carried sewage out to the Thames.

London had a problem getting rid of its rubbish for centuries, and for a long time the East End benefited. There was no mains drainage in the Middle Ages – instead excrement would be stored in cesspits under the houses. This 'nightsoil' would then be carted away to 'laystalls', and then from there to the new market gardens around the Essex villages of Stepney, Bethnal Green and Bow. If that sounds unsanitary, it was an improvement on the earlier system in the City, where a gulley down the middle of the street would be awash with rubbish and human excrement. The lack of concern of Londoners was shown by Samuel Pepys' observation in his *Diary*, recording how his wife 'stooped in the street to do her business'.

The Tower Hamlets market gardens may have flourished, but

Joseph Bazalgette

by the mid-1800s they had been buried under bricks and mortar, and cholera epidemics were sweeping the borough. In desperation, the newly-formed Metropolitan Commission of Sewers decreed in 1847 that cesspits were now banned. The move was a disaster, as the main sewers and underground streams now discharged filth straight into the Thames. A decade before, salmon had been seen jumping in the river at Wapping. By the 1850s nothing could live in what had become nothing less than a huge, stinking open sewer.

The matter came to a head in the long, hot summer of 1858. Wapping windows were draped with lime chloride-soaked curtains, and tons of chalk and carbolic acid were tipped into the Thames. But nothing could mask 'The Great Stink' as it became known. Prime minister Benjamin Disraeli himself described the river as 'a Stygian Pool reeking with ineffable and unbearable horror'. It was the last straw, and in that year a Bill for the purification of the Thames was passed – but the first step was to find an answer to the removal of the waste of three million Londoners.

> "By 1850, the Thames had become a huge open stinking sewer"

One plan was proposed by the painter John 'Mad' Martin. Rather unfairly named, his plan was to pipe the filth out to Essex to propagate land – pretty much what the East Enders had previously done for their farmland. But the task eventually fell to the great engineer Joseph Bazalgette. He constructed a huge system of sewers running east from London Bridge for 11 miles, assisted by pumping stations such as Abbey Mills. By the time Bazalgette was finished, London boasted 1,300 miles of sewers, along with the London Underground, one of the great engineering marvels of his age. And as with the Underground, many still serve East Enders today, albeit creaking and leaking, as shortage of water again engages the minds of Government.

Inventors, Architects and Pioneers

Pickler Platt's fresh ideas

These days, keeping your fruit, veg and meat fresh is easy – you just pop it in the fridge or freezer. As a result, the time-honoured culinary arts of bottling, curing, pickling and salting are performed mainly as a treat for the tastebuds, rather than from hygienic – or economic – necessity. Go back 400 years though, and things were very different. Keeping the abundant spring and autumn harvests fresh to see folk through the long, cold months of winter was a matter of life and death, and throwing food away was a costly luxury. It was to these problems that wealthy Bethnal Green landowner Sir Hugh Platt turned his considerable intellect in the late 1500s.

The son of a successful Hertfordshire brewer, Hugh was also a bright lad, and studied at Cambridge University before coming down to London to study law at Lincoln's Inn. Blessed with an inventive and eccentric streak, Hugh never came to the bar. Instead, he bought a fine country house, Bishops Hall in Bethnal Green, and set about his studies of the cultivation of new and unusual plant varieties. It was the time of Elizabeth I and England's emergence as a naval and imperial power. Adventurers such as Sir Francis Drake were coming back from the new colonies with exotic crops such as tobacco and potatoes and Sir Hugh eagerly set about raising these from his East End soil. He also made wine grown from his own vineyards.

But if the new foods the Navy was bringing back were a source

Sir Hugh Platt

of excitement to Sir Hugh, the problem of keeping that same Navy fed sparked his scientific imagination into life.

The problem was ships had never sailed so far from land, fresh food and clean water. Scurvy and rotten grub were a problem. In his experiments, Hugh discovered keeping fresh fruit in a vacuum prolonged its life – and so was born the bottling of fruit. He also found that boiling beef in brine would stop decay. One of his recipes read as follows: 'To preserve cowcumbers all the yeere: Take a gallon of faire water and a bottle of verjuice, and a pint of bay salt, and a handful of greene fennel or Dill; boile it a little, and when it is cold put it into a barrel, and then put your cowcumbers into that pickle, and you shall keep all the yeere.'

Sir Francis Drake, busy with fitting his ship, the Defiance, broke off from his work at Wapping to see Sir Hugh's work at Bethnal Green. The adventurer was so impressed that he took quantities of Platt's salted meats and bottled fruits on his voyage. Drake also took Sir Hugh's advice on keeping the drinking water fresh – though the addition of powdered brimstone (sulphur) might not be swallowed quite so happily by today's sailors.

> "Platt had found a way to keep the navy in edible supplies"

Platt also addressed the health problems that the new foodstuffs were causing. Rich Londoners of the late 1500s were already developing smoker's coughs and rotten teeth from eating too much sugar – Queen Elizabeth's teeth were black from decay, and he devised toothbrushes and picks. He was also ahead of his time in developing a western version of the Turkish bath. In his 'delicate stove to sweat in', a gentlewoman could 'sit or stand in the steam for two hours or more, her head helde above the tubbe'.

Sir Hugh's authority and knowledge was growing. He drew up plans for English agriculture, advocating crop rotation and the use of artificial fertilisers. He was knighted in 1605, by James I.

Inventors, Architects and Pioneers

An eye for the main chance

Today their name is famous as half of one of Britain's biggest firms of opticians. But centuries ago, Spitalfields family the Dollonds were famed for their precision optical pieces. John Dollond was born into a family of Huguenot immigrants in 1706, and first joined the family business, silk weaving. But in his spare time he worked on his hobbies of optics and astronomy. In the 1750s Dollond, approaching the end of his life, made his name. By now he was running a small optical workshop in Vine Street, Spitalfields, with his son Peter.

In 1747, Isaac Newton stirred up a controversy when he said chromatic aberrations in lenses couldn't be corrected. It meant scientists, soldiers and especially sailors would have to put up with the colour distortions that made their precision spyglasses rather less precise. John Dollond set to in his workshop to prove the great astronomer wrong, and came up with the famed achromatic lens, made of flint and crown glass, for use in telescopes. The invention won him the Royal Society's Copley Medal, but it emerged that Dollond was not the first to come up with the idea.

Twenty years before, a lawyer called Chester More Hall, whose hobby was telescopes, had stumbled on the fact flint glass dispersed colour better than crown glass. Hall reckoned if he glued the concave face of a flint glass lens to the convex face of a crown glass lens, the two would cancel each other's deviations out – no colour dispersion.

John and Peter Dollond

With the growth of maritime trade, telescope makers were doing good business in England at the time, and Hall reckoned that he could be onto a winner. He decided to keep his idea secret until he could hire a lens maker to make his new achromatic lens. Cunningly, he used two different optical shops, one to grind and polish the flint glass lens and the other to make the crown glass lens. But the clever plan foundered when the two shops subcontracted their jobs out to the same lens maker, one George Bass.

Bass was sharp enough to realise the importance of the discovery but not sharp enough to act. Meanwhile, Hall used the lens to make his telescope in the 1730s. But for some reason he never marketed it. Crucially, he failed to patent it either. Amazingly, two men held knowledge that could revolutionise the telescope – a problem exercising minds as great as Newton's – yet for 20 years nobody told anyone.

Forward to the 1750s, and Bass met John Dollond, who was working on his own solution to the problem. Bass told Dollond his story and Dollond created and patented his own version of the lens.

> "Bass failed either to patent or market his design ... a big mistake"

Dollond's reputation grew, and this helped his telescope business. Perfect flint glass was hard to make, and in the late 18th century, glass makers could supply only small quantities. Dollond had first choice, ensuring his shop was supplied with raw materials to produce the most advanced telescopes of the period.

There were many violators of Dollond's patent, but the optician, who died just three years later, in 1761, never prosecuted – perhaps mindful of the source of his 'discovery'. By the 1800s Horatio Nelson and the Duke of Wellington were buying their telescopes from the firm, and the eyepieces came to be known generically as 'Dollonds' much as vacuum cleaners are called 'Hoovers' or you 'Google' results on the web today.

Inventors, Architects and Pioneers

The man who built our piers

The East End has produced its fair share of innovators, inventors, builders and engineers. But it's a fair bet none of them has provided so much seaside fun as Eugenius Birch. Eugenius was born in Gloucester Terrace, Shoreditch on 20 June 1818 to grain dealer John and wife Susanne. From an early age Eugenius was fascinated with the mechanical advances of his age – early Victorian England saw the march of steamships, the railways and the canals that began to criss-cross the country. Living in the East End he was at the heart of this burgeoning transport network. He watched enthralled as the Regent's Canal was cut inland from the Limehouse Basin, and watched the early steamships emerge from East End shipyards.

So inspired was he that when still a boy he submitted a model of a railway carriage to the Greenwich Railway Company. Cleverly, he had put the wheels under the carriages and not on the sides, freeing more room for the passengers. At just 16 Eugenius was employed at Bligh's engineering works in Limehouse, and then joined the Mechanic's Institute. In 1837, the 19-year-old Eugenius received a silver Isis Medal from the Society of Arts for his drawing of a marine steam engine. And he showed a rare gift for draftsmanship too – in 1838 he received a silver medal for his drawings and description of Huddert's rope machinery.

In 1845 Birch went into partnership with his elder brother. Like the other great engineers of the day they didn't specialise in one

Eugenius Birch

area. Soon they were at work building railways, viaducts and bridges, including the Kelham and Stockwith bridges in Nottinghamshire. And, like a good Victorian, he took his work into the Empire, getting involved in the building of the Calcutta-Delhi railway line in India.

But it is for a seemingly trivial branch of his work that Eugenius Birch found fame among the Victorian engineer-inventors. His 14 seaside piers around the coasts of England and Wales were to give delight long after many of his bridges had been demolished and his rail lines terminated. 'The seaside' was hugely fashionable in Victorian Britain. The aristocracy and ordinary East Enders alike took the new rail lines to the coast to escape the smog of London. When a group of Margate businessmen decided to raise the profile of their resort by building a pier in 1853, they handed an open commission to Birch. He brought two innovations to the project. First he imported the Indian styles and decorations he'd absorbed from his time on the sub-continent. And crucially, he introduced screw piles. So strong was this foundation that Margate Pier survived right up to January 1978 when severe storms finally broke it.

"Eugenius's fanciful architectural confections continue to bring joy"

A slew of commissions was to follow as seaside towns realised the pulling power of a pier, including Blackpool North, Aberystwyth, Deal, Homsea, Lytham, Plymouth, New Brighton, Eastbourne, Scarborough, Weston-Super-Mare, Hastings and Bournemouth – and most famous of all, the West Pier at Brighton. Brighton West Pier, with its oriental octagonal kiosks and the long ornate lines of seats was widely admired, and much copied. Today, it's a tumbledown wreck, and was shut in 1975, being further damaged by fire in 2003. But the piles Birch drove into the seabed stand, resisting corrosion from sea and wind.

Inventors, Architects and Pioneers

The man who measured life

The older we get, the greater our risk of dying. This may seem commonsense, but the unwelcome truth was first cast into mathematical form by an amateur East End mathematician. That Benjamin Gompertz ever got the chance to develop his Law of Mortality was down to the help of another long-gone East End institution – the Spitalfields Mathematical Society. The Gompertz family were merchants who – like many others in the late 1700s – left Holland to try their luck in a London booming with trade. Three brothers were born in the new family home, in Spitalfields, with Benjamin arriving in 1779. The young Gompertz showed a prodigious ability in mathematics, but there was a major obstacle. The family was Jewish, meaning Benjamin was denied entrance to university.

He set about educating himself, learning mathematics by reading Newton and Maclaurin. But an extraordinary East End institution was soon to give him a helping hand. The Spitalfields Mathematical Society met in pubs around the East End and, crucially, anyone could join in. There was just one rule. Anyone receiving tuition from the Society had to make himself available in turn as a tutor. If a fellow member asked a question, their colleague had to try to find an answer – or pay a fine of a penny.

Gompertz was browsing in a bookshop and got chatting to the bookseller, one John Griffiths, and a member of the Society. The two became friends and Griffiths saw to it his talented discovery

Benjamin Gompertz

was elected to the Society, although at 18 he was three years below the official age of entry.

In 1810 Gompertz married Abigail Montefiore, who came from a wealthy Jewish family with strong links with the Stock Exchange. Gompertz himself joined the Stock Exchange in 1810 and became a Fellow of the Royal Society in 1819. The following year he read a paper to the Society which applied differential calculus to the calculation of life expectancy. In short he was working out, for every age of a person, how likely they were to die. The seeds of Gompertz's Law of Mortality had been sown.

Gompertz was now marrying his mathematical brilliance to the cold science of insurance, and in 1824 he was appointed as actuary and head clerk of the Alliance Assurance Company.

And in 1825, he observed that after the age of 20, there was a doubling of the 'force of mortality' every seven years. The Gompertz equation reflected the cellular and molecular deterioration that pushes us towards disease and death.

This geometric progression led to the plotting of a straight line, known as the Gompertz function. Gompertz

"Marrying maths and insurance, Gompertz worked out when you would die"

had plotted the actuarial principles which underpin life assurance to this day. It's the reason your premiums go up and your dividends go down as you get older. Buy life assurance and someone, somewhere, is looking at the Gompertz function ... and working out how likely it is you'll see the year out. So the next time you're horrified at the cost of renewing your insurance, curse East End boy Benjamin Gompertz.

Ironically, Gompertz himself was to go off the scale. He lived to the ripe old age of 86 – which would horrify the actuaries. He died in 1865 and outlived the Spitalfields Mathematical Society by nearly 20 years.

Inventors, Architects and Pioneers

Shifting the axis of London

In 1800, Parliament passed an Act to authorise the building of the West India Docks. The City took the opportunity to relieve the crowded Thames by siting the new dock downriver on the Isle of Dogs. Amazingly, the dock took just two years to complete, testament to the organisational brilliance of architect John Rennie.

But although Rennie was to become, the most celebrated civil engineer of his age, it was from unlikely beginnings. Rennie was born a farmer's son on 7 June, 1761, in East Lothian. It was a lucky chance that the innovative engineer, Andrew Meikle, had his workshop nearby. John would visit the works, and soon began making models of the complex mechanisms he saw there. By ten he was producing miniature windmills and steam engines.

But the precocious talent wasn't satisfied in erecting windmills for local farmers. He moved to Edinburgh University, where he studied natural philosophy (science) and chemistry. With a recommendation from his Edinburgh tutor, he was taken into the employment of James Watt, in Soho. On his journey south, Rennie took the opportunity of examining some of the new engineering wonders of the day – the aqueduct bridge at Lancaster, the docks at Liverpool, and the works on the Bridgewater canal.

Watt gave the young apprentice the job of designing and building the Albion flour mills in Blackfriars. Completed in 1789, the work displayed Rennie's characteristic skills. Replacing the con-

John Rennie

ventional wooden gears with robust iron, the engineering was precise, the workmanship tidy, and the mills superbly efficient and productive. Even the rather paranoid Watt, who was often jealous of the work of others, had to admit Rennie's thoroughness. It was an attention to detail that was to make his work expensive, but soon Rennie was promoted to become manager of the works.

Rennie embarked on a career of staggering diversity and industry. From the 1790s, he carved out canals such as the Aberdeen, the Great Western, the Kennet and Avon, the Portsmouth, the Birmingham, and the Worcester. He designed docks at Hull, Leith, Greenock, Liverpool, and Dublin. And he built harbours at Berwick, Dunleary (Dun Laoghaire), Howth, Newhaven, and Queensferry.

And it was on the back of this massive outpouring of work that his commission (with William Jessop) came for the West India Docks, soon followed by work on the London Docks at Wapping, in 1805.

The effect of John Rennie's work on the East End is incalculable. Now it was the centre for London's maritime trade, with new roads being driven to the area, and hamlets such as Poplar mushrooming in size. His work on Britain's canal infrastructure meant goods could more quickly be dispersed around the country and so became cheaper and more plentiful, stimulating the economy of east London.

> "Rennie shifted London's trade to the east ... the city was changed forever"

In 1811, Rennie began building Waterloo Bridge, at a cost of more than £1 million. He then planned the Southwark Bridge, built of his favoured cast iron. And most famously, he was to design a new London Bridge. It's probably Rennie's most famous monument though he died before work even started. He died in 1821, of inflammation of the liver, and it was left to his sons, George and John Rennie, to build their father's London Bridge.

Inventors, Architects and Pioneers

A genius for self destruction

Robert Hooke was one of the most gifted men of his age. His misfortune was to live in the same age as Isaac Newton and Christopher Wren, pushing Hooke into the historical shadows. Hooke's place in East End history is sealed by his design for the rebuilding of the infamous Bedlam hospital, eventually demolished to make way for Liverpool Street rail station in the 1870s. But Hooke achieved much more, being architect, scientist, inventor and working closely with his friend Wren on building a new London in the wake of the Great Fire.

Hooke was born the son of a curate at All Saints Church in Freshwater on the Isle of Wight, in 1635. Here his father John ran a small school attached to the church. Nobody expected Robert to reach maturity. Constantly sick, he suffered blinding headaches which made studying hard; the boy was excused lessons and left to his own devices. But if he had a weak body, Robert had a keen eye and brain. He made detailed sketches of the plants, animals, farms, rocks, cliffs and sea of the island. And he was fascinated by mechanical toys and clocks. Observing a watchmaker dismantling and fixing the family timepiece, Robert built his own clock, entirely from wooden parts. The boy began to view nature itself as a complex machine, and determined to unlock its secrets.

Moving to London, Hooke enrolled at Westminster School, and had read the first six books of Euclid's *Elements* by the end of his first week. He then quickly worked his way through the school

Robert Hooke

library, learning Latin and Greek and especially geometry. Music was another interest and he learnt to play the organ. In 1653, he felt he had learned all he could at school, and entered Christ College, Oxford where he won a chorister's place. There was an explosion of talent at Oxford at that time, with Thomas Willis, Seth Ward, Robert Boyle, John Wilkins, John Wallis, Christopher Wren and William Petty meeting as the 'philosophical college'. Hooke learnt astronomy from Ward and Wilkins gave him a copy of his *Mathematical Magick*, on mechanical geometry.

Leaving Oxford, Hooke went to work with Boyle, who had him construct an air pump. The design devised is the basis for pumps to this day. Simultaneously he was thinking about how clocks could measure longitude at sea, to develop a timepiece based on springs rather than pendulums. But though it could have made him a fortune, when Hooke realised a patent would allow anyone who improved on his design to receive royalties, he sulkily scrapped the work. This attitude would blight his later years.

At the height of fame, Hooke was to undergo a long and bitter

"His brilliance ignored, Robert Hooke was written out of history at a stroke"

decline – partly of his own making. Isaac Newton produced a theory of light and colour in 1672 to general acclaim. But Hooke claimed the good bits were stolen from his own work, while the original bits were wrong. Picking a fight with the most brilliant and ambitious scientist England had ever seen was a tactically disastrous move. Newton removed all reference to Hooke – once a friend - from his *Principia*.

Hooke died in 1703. Written out of the history books, he was described as a 'lean, bent and ugly man'. For centuries it was believed he avoided having his portrait painted – none were found and some grotesque hook-nosed cartoons had to stand in their stead.

Inventors, Architects and Pioneers

Architect who broke the rules

Nicholas Hawksmoor was an architect who never found the fame of his employers and mentors Vanbrugh and Wren. For many years he was considered less an architect than a 'mere' mason, putting Wren and Vanbrugh's ideas into practice, yet embellishing them with extraordinary elements of his own style. But over the last few years, the original, sometimes bizarre work of Hawksmoor has been gaining new recognition.

Born to a Nottinghamshire farming family in 1661, Hawksmoor became fascinated by architecture early. At 18 he left home to work in London as a clerk for Sir Christopher Wren, the Surveyor General. He was a quick learner and soaked up the skills of his master. From 1684 Hawksmoor worked with Wren on all his big projects: Chelsea Hospital, St. Paul's Cathedral, Hampton Court Palace, and Greenwich Hospital. And around the turn of the century Hawksmoor began to work with the other great architect of the day, John Vanbrugh, helping build Blenheim Palace and Castle Howard.

Unlike his contemporaries, Hawksmoor didn't take the traditional route of travelling to Italy to observe classical architecture at first hand. Instead, his version of the classical style was formed by his extensive library. But his reading didn't stop with the strict classical orders and the work of Palladio. Instead he drew from his study of the larger ancient world – from the pyramids, the Temple of Solomon and many more.

Nicholas Hawksmoor

The architect found himself at odds with the fashions of the day. The dominant Palladian style took cues from the neo-classical work of Italian architect Palladio, and demanded every building conform to the 'orders' of architecture in Ancient Greece (at least as seen through the eyes of 18th century British architects). 'Where they fancy too much liberty is taken they call it Gothick,' Hawksmoor complained furiously of the narrowmindedness of his contemporaries.

When it came to commissions for rebuilding London's churches after the Great Fire, Hawksmoor happily went on taking liberties, topping monumental towers with satyrs, giant flowering clumps of stone, enormous scrolls and, most of all, pyramids. The three East End churches of St George, St Anne and Christ Church (recently restored) were superb buildings and awash with references and metaphor. The original plan was for 50 churches to be built, of which our trio were just the first. In the event only a handful were built before the money ran out. And this was just part of a much grander plan. Wren drew up a plan for the entire rebuilding of London. There would be an ordered grid of roads, with monumental civic buildings such as the halls of the City Companies, the Customs House and St Paul's Cathedral at the hubs of radial streets.

"He despaired at the narrow vision of other architects"

Both Wren and Hawksmoor sought to emphasise the social value of public buildings. 'It establishes a nation, draws people and commerce; makes the people love their native country' believed the older man. But instead, wrote Hawksmoor 'We have no city, nor streets, nor houses, but a chaos of dirty rotten sheds, always tumbling or taking fire, with winding crooked passages, lakes of mud and rills of stinking mire running through them'.

For the boy born just before the Great Fire, and who had dreamed of a beautiful new London rising from the ashes, it was a tragically missed opportunity.

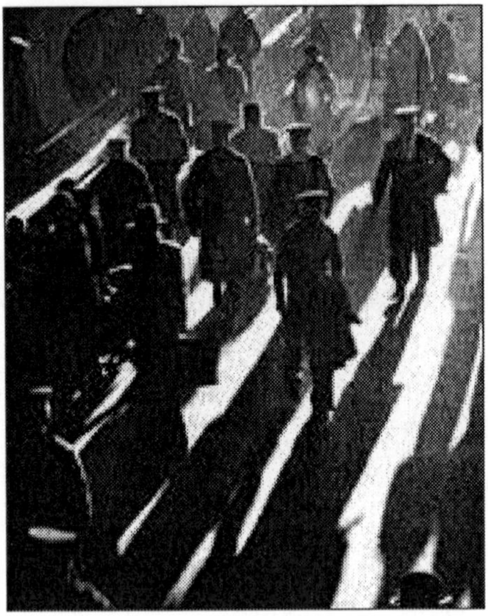

Eccentrics, mystics and charlatans

Joseph Druce 174, The Tichborne Claimant 176, Eliza Marchpane 178, The Blind Beggar 180; The Mad Hatter 182; Charlie Brown.

Eccentrics, Mystics and Charlatans

Limehouse's Maori chief

For centuries, the people of the East End have been travelling to the four corners of the globe as sailors, traders, missionaries and colonists. And for centuries they have been returning from distant lands, bringing cargoes, customs, new words and new ideas that have enriched London and made it the cosmopolitan city it is today. Many have returned with extraordinary tales and with new found riches from their travels but the story of Joseph Druce must be one of the most amazing.

Druce came from a humble enough beginning. He was born in 1777 in Shadwell, the son of a labourer in a Limehouse distillery. The young Joseph moved from job to job, working on fishing boats out of the Thames and spending a short time in Bellamy's Ropeworks. But he fell into trouble when he turned to crime. And in March 1791, he was convicted of housebreaking and robbery at the Old Bailey.

The usual sentence was hanging: in the late 1700s hundreds of Britons, including children, were hanged every year for such petty offences as shoplifting and pickpocketing. But Joseph was lucky to come up before a 'liberal' judge. He was sentenced to death, but because he was only 13 the sentence was commuted to transportation to the colonies. So, like thousands of his fellow Englishmen in the 18th and 19th centuries, Druce began the long and perilous voyage to New South Wales, Australia.

Transportation was seen as a cheap and final way of England

Joseph Druce, Maori Chief

getting rid of its problems. Many of the convicts did not survive the journey, with its storms, scurvy and sickness. But Druce survived and did quite well in his new home, working as a bushranger and, ironically, a police officer.

However, the sea soon beckoned again and he signed up on one of the many merchant ships running the route between Australia and New Zealand. On one of his journeys, he met and befriended a Maori chief. His new friend became sick on the journey and Joseph nursed him to health, returning him to his grateful family in New Zealand.

The Maoris had settled in New Zealand around a thousand years before after completing an epic sea journey from Hawaiki, in Polynesia. They had lived peacefully for centuries but when the Europeans arrived, they brought conflict with them. The Maoris found themselves driven from their traditional lands and endured appalling treatment at the hands of the settlers, the indigenous race being almost wiped out. But Joseph found himself welcomed by a hospitable people – so welcome, in fact, that he married his new friend's daughter. And the poor boy from Limehouse found himself created a fully-fledged Maori chief.

> "He was, by turns, thief, policeman, sailor, Maori chief and author"

Sadly, his wife didn't live, and Joseph put their baby daughter into an orphanage. He was a free man, having been pardoned in 1801, and he joined the HMS Porpoise, setting sail for London. Back home, he fell on hard times again and, in 1851, there is a record of his entering the Shadwell Workhouse. At 40, the ailing Joseph was taken in to the Greenwich Seamen's Hospital where he revealed a final talent – producing the story of his extraordinary life, *The Life of a Greenwich Pensioner*. In 1819 Joseph died. Sailor, policeman, author and Maori chief – in 42 years he had lived enough lives for half a dozen men.

Eccentrics, Mystics and Charlatans

The Tichborne claimant

Arthur Orton wasn't a man born to great things but the Wapping butcher knew he wanted more than a lifetime selling sausages. In 1852 18-year-old Arthur set sail for Australia, a new identity and one of the most costly, lengthy and extraordinary trials in legal history.

In the New World, peers and paupers could rub shoulders as equals and Arthur befriended the exiled Sir Alfred Tichborne, the 11th Baronet. Alfred died in 1866 but confided in Arthur the Tichborne family secrets, not least the 'loss' of his elder brother Roger. Sir Roger Doughty Tichborne had been born in Paris in 1829, 10 years before Alfred. And, after receiving his military commission in the Sixth Dragoons, he was expected to become the 11th baronet. But Roger disliked military life, preferring to fritter the family fortune in the clubs of London with his friends. He also had an eye for the ladies and soon a romance was blossoming with one Katherine Doughty. Her parents were appalled, not least by the fact that the dissolute Tichborne was Katherine's first cousin.

The parents decided on a three-year wait before the two exchanged vows, reckoning that the feckless Tichborne would lose interest. The plan suited Roger perfectly, and he immediately made plans for a world tour. The 24-year-old peer set sail for Rio de Janeiro in January 1853. From there he journeyed to New York, setting off on the SS Bella on 20 April 1854. Young

Arthur Orton

Tichborne never reached the US, the vessel capsizing due to a poorly balanced load of coffee. Around 40 passengers and crew were presumed lost when an empty lifeboat was found drifting a by a passing ship.

Roger's younger brother stood in line to inherit Tichborne wealth. But young Alfred was, if anything, even more feckless than his brother. His mother, Lady Henrietta was determined he should not succeed his father. Clutching at straws, and the rumour that Roger had survived the wreck, Henrietta placed advertisements in newspapers inviting information about her son's whereabouts.

Glancing over a week old copy of the Times in a shanty hut in Wagga Wagga, Australia, Orton's eye chanced on the name Tichborne. Orton had not only met the late baronet but Sir Edward Doughty's valet Bogle. Orton decided on a bold gamble. Using Bogle as a go-between he travelled to Melbourne and passed himself off as Roger. He returned to London, at Lady Henrietta's expense, to meet his 'mum'.

"Lady Henrietta convinced herself he was Roger"

Bizarrely, Lady Henrietta convinced herself an obese man with an Australian accent was her slim, aesthetic and aristocratic son but other members of the family were not so easily fooled. The case went before the London Court of Common Pleas on 11 May 1871. Three years, hundreds of witnesses and 10,000 pages of evidence later, the prosecution found Orton's claim false. That he had forgotten any details of the first 16 years of his life and no longer had his schooldays' tattoo of the initials RCT on his arm were just two damning pieces of evidence. Orton got 14 years, serving 10 before release in 1884. In poverty he sold his story to *People* magazine and he died on April Fool's Day 1898.

The imposter was buried in a coffin bearing the legend: Sir Roger Charles Doughty Tichborne. It seems the only person he fooled was himself..

The marzipan madame

Christmas is a time of tradition and indulgence. A stuffed goose has given way to the turkey and Christmas pudding is a popular choice instead of plum duff. But one thing remains – Yuletide is a time of feasting, and dining on delicacies we never really eat for the rest of the year.

The centrepiece of any Christmas is the cake, with its rich casing of marzipan. The soft yellow paste had been a rare luxury in Europe for centuries before it caught on here. How it did so is a remarkable story, for marzipan owes its popularity and its very name to a poor girl from Stepney who fled the East End for fame and fortune.

Eliza Marchpane was born in 1760 and, like thousands of other girls born in Stepney that year, faced a miserable life of drudgery, poverty, marriage – if she was lucky – followed by a huge brood of children. Then, if she were lucky, her almost-certain early demise would be a peaceful and painless one. Of course one way to scrape a living was to follow the tradition of countless other cockney girls of the time, and become a prostitute, working the inns of Wapping and Ratcliff. That was the path Eliza took. But, looking around her at the women who had been plying the trade for a dozen years, she realised she would be old before her time and her value would fade.

She decided to move upmarket. Saving her money, she bought a passage onboard a ship to the continent. In Paris she purchased

Eliza Marchpane

a single set of fine clothes and adopted the title 'Marquesa de Marchpane'. In England, her accent had marked her out as a guttersnipe. To unaccustomed ears in the salons and boudoirs of Europe, she sounded strange and exotic.

The beautiful Eliza moved around the courts of Europe, becoming a famed courtesan, with a string of aristocratic lovers swelling her fortune. In the 1790s she came to Vienna, where she seduced the young musical genius Mozart, composer of *The Marriage of Figaro* and *The Magic Flute*. And it was in Vienna, the most fashionable city in Europe at the time, that she first tasted little delicacies fashioned from almond paste.

Eliza was back in London at the turn of the 19th century, but she certainly wasn't going to revisit Stepney. 'The Marquesa de Marchpane' was rich and established and had a 'foreign' accent by way of disguise. She set up home in the affluent West End, where she gave dinner parties and soirees. The exotic and beautiful Continental courtesan was a huge hit and her parties boasted many dishes and delicacies imported from Europe – among them the little sweets and fruits made from 'marchpane', or marzipan as it become known.

> "She came back to London, Stepney accent erased"

Marzipan became a delicacy – sugar and almonds were expensive and made it the province of the rich.

By the time Eliza died in Brighton in 1830, she had been the lover of the dandified and promiscuous Prince Regent, the future George IV, and marzipan was fast becoming an integral part of Christmas. And when Charles Dickens penned his descriptions of 'traditional' English Yule feasts 20 years later, the marzipan-clad Christmas cake was a firm – and cheap – popular favourite.

Eliza had fulfiled her aim, to escape poverty and an early death, to find riches. But with all her rich imagination, she could never have dreamed of her legacy to our Christmas a century later.

Eccentrics, Mystics and Charlatans

Blind Beggar of Bethnal Green

He gave his name to one of the most infamous, pubs in Britain. But who exactly was the Blind Beggar of Bethnal Green? The story itself is shrouded in legend, and set in a Bethnal Green vastly different from the chaotic and overcrowded slum it became in the 19th century.

Bethnal Green is first mentioned in an Eighth Century deed. One Mathilda le Vayre of Stepney is listed as having a home in 'Blithehall', and making a grant of the house's courtyard. By the Middle Ages, Bethnal Green was isolated from London, a quiet little village and rather grand. There were mansions in the surrounding countryside and cottages were clustered around the green itself.

In the 1200s, one of those manor houses belonged to Simon de Montford, a young lord today commemorated by Montford House, a red-brick block of flats on the north side of Victoria Park Square. His story, and how he went from landed gentry to poor beggar, became hugely popular in early Tudor times, and was revived by Percy's *Reliques of Ancient English Poetry*, published in 1765.

Simon was a soldier in the service of the king, and fought at the Battle of Evesham, in the West Country, in 1265. According to the legend, he fell at the battle and was found wandering, blinded, by a nobleman's daughter. She nursed the wounded soldier back to health, they fell in love and were married.

The Blind Beggar of Bethnal Green

In time a daughter arrived, but although Besse was beautiful she couldn't find a husband – the problem being her father. Besse was courted by four suitors; a rich gentleman, a knight, a London merchant and the son of an innkeeper. Most withdrew their suit when they met Montford to ask for the old soldier's consent.

Montford's reduced circumstances were related through a popular song of the time: 'My father, shee said, is soone to be seene, The siely, blind beggar of Bednall-green, That daylye sits begging for charitie, He is the good father of pretty Besse. Hie marks and his tokens are knowen very well; He always is led with a dogg and a bell; A seely old man, God knoweth, is he, Yet he is the father of pretty Besse.'

In a predictably medieval twist, the courtly knight was the only man who could see past the seeming lack of a decent dowry to the woman he loved. He received his reward, as the couple received a dowry of £3,000, plus £100 for Besse's wedding dress.

The legend persisted. Samuel Pepys visited fashionable Bethnal Green to stay with his friend, Sir William Ryder. 'This very house was built by the Blind Beggar of Bednall-green, so much talked of and sang in ballads,' recorded Pepys.

"By the 18th century the Blind Beggar symbol was everywhere around the East End"

By 1690, the Bethnal Green beadle bore the badge of the Blind Beggar on his ceremonial staff. And in the 18th century every pub in the area bore the image of the beggar on their signs. Kirby's Castle, a lunatic asylum, was dubbed the Blind Beggar's House in 1727.

But Besse is remembered in Besse Street, the mayor bears an image of Simon and Besse on the borough's ceremonial badge and, most famous of all, in 1966, the Kray twins and the unfortunate George Cornell sealed the Blind Beggar (the final pub to bear the badge) in the nation's folklore forever.

Eccentrics, Mystics and Charlatans

The original Mad Hatter

These days you'd be hard pushed to be a hermit in Bethnal Green. But 300 years ago, when it was a sleepy hamlet, buried in the countryside a couple of miles east of the London wall, it was a different matter. For the East End was home to a recluse who became an inspiration for Lewis Carroll's Mad Hatter: whose strange tale brought together Alice in Wonderland and Oliver Cromwell, religion, astrology, medicine and fortune telling.

Roger Crab was originally a Buckinghamshire man and a soldier. He enlisted in the English army, what was to become the New Model Army of Oliver Cromwell, in 1642. England was in turmoil, embroiled in the series of battles running from 1639 to 1660 which would become collectively known as the English Civil War. The hands-on rule of Charles I was infuriating Parliament, as was his habit of levying taxes without the permission of the Commons.

Crab signed up in 1642, just as Parliament and Charles had fallen out yet again, this time over who should raise an army to put down the Irish rebellion. The King, affronted at the challenge to his authority, tried to marshal the provinces against a London heavily favouring the Roundheads. He failed, and it was Cromwell who raised the force to viciously suppress the Irish.

Crab was a good soldier. Standing a full 6ft 7in – a giant by today's standards, let alone those of the 17th century – he terrified the men he fought against. Over the next few years, he travelled with the Roundheads as they crushed revolts in Ireland and Scotland and, for the first time, England totally dominated the British Isles. But the next challenge was to come from within England. There were constant battles between Royalist and Republican forces, especially following the execution of Charles in 1649. The battles of Edgehill, Naseby, Newbury, Marston Moor and the rest peppered the 1640s. But it was probably in the battle for Colchester in 1648 that Crab received the knock that was to change his life forever.

The soldier was badly stunned by a blow on the head from a Royalist soldier. The injury led to early discharge from the army and he returned to Chesham, where he set up in business as a hatter. He was a success but the blow was affecting Crab. He sold the firm and gave his money to the poor, and took up residence in a tree near Uxbridge. The former puritan began to dabble in astrology and 'physic' or natural medicine. His philosophy was confused but had its roots in a rejection of conventional religion. The soldier became a pacifist, and moved to secluded Bethnal Green, where he lived on three farthings a week, eating grass, mallow and dock leaves.

> "He lived in secluded Bethnal Green on grass and dock leaves"

Crab developed a talent for telling the future. Ironically, one of his visions was that the monarchy would be restored and, in 1660, Charles took the throne as Charles II. The diet of grass did the old man's health no harm. He lived to 79, dying in 1680. He is remembered on his tomb in Stepney's St Dunstan's churchyard with this epitaph. 'Through good and ill reports he past, oft censured, yet approved at last ... a friend to everything that's good.' And he was remembered 200 years later, when Lewis Carroll based his Mad Hatter character in *Alice's Adventures in Wonderland* on Crab.

Eccentrics, Mystics and Charlatans

Odd legacy of Charlie Brown

IT is a familiar landmark to any Londoner driving back from Essex, and anyone taking the M11 motorway up to Stansted will have passed over it. But from where did the Charlie Brown's roundabout, one of London's busiest intersections, get its unusual name? The roundabout was named after a larger-than-life Limehouse man. Yet how did the bland and featureless junction come to be connected with one of the East End's most colourful characters?

The story begins in the 1890s when Charlie Brown, a former boxer, took over the ownership of the Railway Tavern. The Limehouse pub stood on the corner of Garford Street and the East India Dock Road and it was a popular watering hole for the sailors and dockers who made up most of Limehouse's population at the time. Even among his noisy and outspoken clientele – many of whom were colourful characters with tales to tell – Charlie managed to stand out.

In fact, he was such a loud and extrovert landlord that he managed to stamp his personality on the pub itself. As Charlie's reputation grew, so did the contents of the pub. Sailors would return from their travels with mementoes from every corner of the globe and bring them back to a delighted guv'nor, who would hang them on the wall of the tavern.

And as the collection grew, its fame spread throughout the capital. People would make the trip down to infamous Limehouse,

Charlie Brown

which in the early 1900s was synonymous with Chinatown, white slaving and opium dens in the public imagination, just to view his map of the world.

In June 1932 Charlie Brown died and the 'uncrowned king of Limehouse' was laid in state in the pub that had been his palace. His funeral procession was fit for a king too, as 16,000 people went to Bow Cemetery to say goodbye to Charlie. Charlie Brown's legacy was a lucrative one, and both his children ran pubs. His daughter Esther kept the existing hostelry, while Charlie Brown Jr was the landlord of the Blue Posts, directly opposite the Railway Hotel. Both of them erected signs saying that their pubs were the genuine Charlie Brown's.

In 1938 Charlie Jr gave up on the East End to move to leafier Woodford, taking the name with him of course. The new Charlie Brown's lay at the end of the Southend to London road which was to become the A127. But in 1972 the road that had given the pub its reason for being also became the cause of its demise, when the road intersection was extended and the pub had to be demolished.

> **"His only memorial is a traffic blackspot on the edge of London**

Young Charlie had salvaged many of the famous mementoes from his dad's pub, and legend has it they passed on to the Greyhound pub in Harlow, though there is no trace of them today.

By a strange coincidence, it was transport that had both created and destroyed the original Charlie Brown's boozer too. The Railway Hotel had first been built to serve the old London and Blackwall Railway in the 1800s. When the Docklands Light Railway was built in 1989, the Railway Tavern stood in the way of the Commercial Road extension and so had to be demolished itself. Today, all that remains of the world-famous character, three pubs and a confusion of names is a traffic blackspot on the fringes of London.

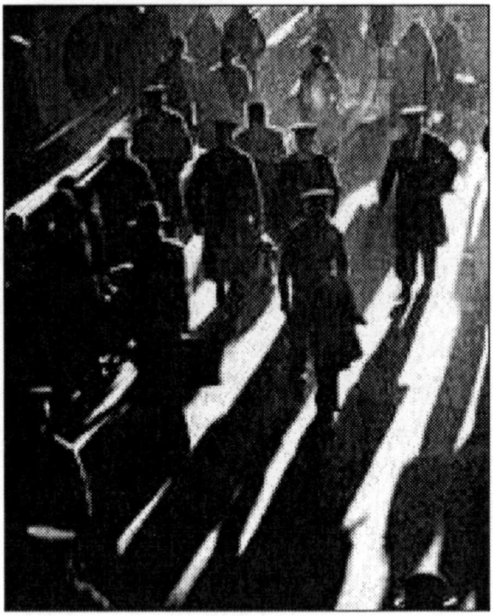

Designers, painters and photographers

The Cockney Snappers 188; Barber Beaumont 190; Mark Gertler 192; William Holman Hunt 194; John Edwards and Francis Bacon 196; William Larkins 198; CR Ashbee 200; Abram Games 202.

Designers, Painters and Photographers

Short, fat and heterosexual

Forty years ago, Swinging London was yet to swing. Everything was in black and white and, in class-bound Britain, fashion photographers were tradesmen – polite, smart, seen but not heard. A new breed of snappers changed all that – Terry O'Neill, Brian Duffy, David Bailey and Terence Donovan. Bailey and Donovan, two kids from the East End, became probably the most celebrated photographers of glamourous women the Sixties produced. Both men started their careers in the West End studio of the doyen of fashion photographers – John French. They were a blast of fresh air, sweeping away the genteel atmosphere of the Forties and Fifties.

Brian Duffy remarked on the culture shock the three were to the business. 'Before 1960, a fashion photographer was tall, thin and camp. But we three are different: short, fat and heterosexual!' And they were working class. A decade before they would probably have had to conceal their roots – in the Sixties they could celebrate them. In between fashion shoots for *Vogue*, and portraits of the characters that made Sixties Britain a creative and artistic powerhouse, Donovan was continually returning to Stepney. The idea of leaving the city he loved for a home in the country appalled him. 'What do I do with it?' he demanded. 'I don't want to take a picture of it, and I don't want to walk in it.'

So he would come back to Stepney each Sunday to see his aunts and uncles, and to revisit the sites of his youth. Taking his

O'Neill, Duffy, Bailey and Donovan

camera he travelled alone round the streets of his childhood – shooting the bombsites, the docks, the cobbled streets and the characters of an East End that was soon to disappear as the developers moved in.

Bailey was doing the same. His early attempts to snap his East End surroundings, on a battered box Brownie, had been a failure. He'd got his first decent camera when he was on National Service in Singapore. And by the Sixties he was at the top of his trade, having broken free of the career path he dreaded. 'If you came from the East End there were only three things you could become – a boxer, a car thief, or maybe a musician,' he joked.

Donovan, too, was grateful he'd broken through the horizons of his childhood, continually surprised he wasn't 'down at Tate and Lyle's loading sugar'. And in the Sixties, in between fashion shoots of his muse Jean Shrimpton, of Twiggy, of the Rolling Stones and the Beatles, Bailey too would often return to Tower Hamlets with his camera. It became business as well as pleasure. His set of pictures for the *Sunday Times* in 1968, East End Faces, was a technicolor record of local life, pubs, clubs and kid boxers – among them a youthful 'Johnny' (later to become John H) Stracey. Most famously of all, Bailey became a wedding photographer for the day, doing the honours at Reggie Kray's wedding to Frances Shea in Bethnal Green.

> "The old East End is gone. I just wish I'd taken more pctures"

The worldwide fashion shoots for the likes of *Vogue* go on to this day for Bailey. Donovan was still photographing the world's most beautiful women in couture's most expensive clothes until his death in 1996. The judo expert committed suicide while depressed as a result of steroids he was taking to treat a skin condition. The East End they continually recorded is, sadly, largely gone. 'It was a kind of innocence,' says Bailey. 'But it's all gone now. My regret is not taking more pictures at the time.'

Designers, Painters and Photographers

Patron of the People's Palace

Each summer, students of Queen Mary, University of London gather at an imposing building on Mile End Road to collect their degree certificates. Few could know that the building they are nervously gathered in boasts one of the longest and strangest histories of any in the East End.

Our story starts back in 1774, when Barber Beaumont was born in Marylebone. The young man showed talent as an artist and was enrolled in the Royal Academy School. It was the beginning of a colourful and varied career. Beaumont's speciality was miniature portraits and he became the court painter to the Duke of Kent and the Duke of York. But the talented artist gave up his painting, making his fortune from insurance after founding the County Fire Office.

Spurred on by his success, and by a philanthropic urge to help the poor of London, Beaumont set up the Provident Life Institute and Bank of Savings. This was one of the first friendly societies, which encouraged working people to save money, the forerunner of modern building societies.

Though a talented and prudent man, Beaumont was a colourful character. He fought a duel in Hyde Park, and left insurance to became a military commander during the Napoleonic Wars. Returning to England, Beaumont set his mind again to philanthropic works. He became determined to bring culture to the East End, by building a combined museum, concert hall and library.

Barber Beaumont

And so, the Eastern Athanaeum was born in Beaumont Square. But his real legacy was a trust fund he endowed to build a home for higher education in east London. The money was released on his death in 1841, but it was to be 40 years before his dream came to reality.

In 1887, Beaumont's educational establishment, known as the People's Palace, was opened by Queen Victoria. It was her first visit to the East End in four decades. Built on the old Bancroft Hospital site, the plan was to include a technical college, gymnasium and swimming pool, library and concert hall. Aimed at the mind as well as the body, it would fulfil Beaumont's dream of 'the intellectual improvement and rational recreation and amusement for people living in the East End of London'.

Thousands turned out to watch the Queen in her rare outings east of the City. And for almost a century, thousands eagerly attended the lectures and classes at the People's Palace and Queen's Hall. But in 1931 disaster struck. Fire ravaged the Palace, the worst of it centred on the Queen's Hall. Two-hundred and fifty firemen fought the blaze and two hours later the fire was out. Little had been saved and the Queen's Hall lay in smouldering ruins.

> "Insurance man and painter, he fought duels and helped the poor"

The East End could have been downhearted, but local Labour MP George Lansbury put his usual positive spin on the disaster. Broadcasting on the radio in 1936, he said: 'We all felt a personal loss, but we were not dismayed. We knew that the goodwill that created our People's Palace was not dead, that all classes of people would readily respond.' And respond they did. An appeal for funds culminated in King George VI and Queen Elizabeth following in the footsteps of the King's great grandmother, Victoria. On 13 February 1937, the King laid the foundation stone of a new People's Palace.

Designers, Painters and Photographers

Torture of an artistic genius

The tortured artist, never sure of his own ability while hailed as a genius by others, is a familiar figure. For Mark Gertler, born into desperate poverty in Spitalfields, but hailed as one of the greatest painters of the early 20th century, it was a terrible contradiction, and one that would lead to suicide.

Gertler was born in 1891, the child of Austrian-Jewish parents. With the family struggling to make ends meet, Mark had to leave school and become a breadwinner at an early age. So it was that he became apprenticed to a stained-glass maker. But he was already showing a keen interest in art and, in spare hours, attended classes at Regent Street Polytechnic.

His teachers were quick to spot the youngster's promise, but to leave regular paid work and pursue a career in art was an impossible dream. Gertler's case was brought to the attention of Sir William Rothenstein, who persuaded the Jewish Education Aid Society to grant Gertler a scholarship for the famed Slade School of Art.

But if Gertler's artistic talent was precociously obvious, so was the mental instability that would dog him for the rest of his short life. In 1906, in his first months at the polytechnic, he started to suffer long nights of sleeplessness and days of depression. Still, from 1909 to 1912 he worked, and shone, at the Slade. Despite the presence of luminous contemporaries such as Dora Carrington, Paul Nash and CRW Nevinson, Gertler won the first

Mark Gertler

prize for Head Painting. Gertler may have been plagued by insecurities but was accepted for his talent by the Bloomsbury set. It was a relationship painted in the 1995 film *Carrington*, starring Emma Thompson as Dora and Rufus Sewell as Mark. They came from very different social circles – the upper-class Carrington, Nash and Lytton Strachey, and the poor immigrant from Spitalfields – but Gertler drew on the East End to give terrifying power to his work.

Gertler's painting *Rabbi and Daughter* (1912) looked back to his childhood. But as he worked among the falling bombs of the first air raids in 1914 and 1915, the horror of the Great War started to permeate his work. In 1916 he finished his masterpiece, **Merry Go Round** in which he seemed to be drawing on and pulling all the strands of his short life together.

'With its harsh flickering restlessness, the painting seemed to be a comment on Mark's life: Whitechapel slum, young artist's Bohemia, fashionable society, the Garsington intelligentsia,' wrote critic William Rothenstein. 'It was impossible, too, to look at these mechanical soldiers going round and round without recalling the horrors of the deadlocked Western Front.'

"He found it hard to discern worth in his own work"

The painting had a stunning effect on people. DH Lawrence wrote: 'Your terrible and beautiful picture is great and true, but horrible and terrifying. I'm not sure I wouldn't be too frightened to look at the original.' But Gertler still spoke of his insecurities. To Rothenstein, he wrote in 1925: 'You ask what is the matter with me? It is the greatest crisis of my life. What is my value as an artist? Is there anything there worthwhile after all?'

Gertler's mental state was not aided by poor health, dating from childhood. He suffered from TB throughout his life, constantly in and out of sanatoriums. And in 1939, with war on the horizon, Gertler, with his early successes behind him, took his own life.

Designers, Painters and Photographers

Middle East in the East End

When William Holman Hunt died in 1910, it brought to an end a painting career begun more than 60 years before – a career which had brought him renown for historical scenes and tableaux from the Bible and the Holy Lands.

Hunt travelled to the Middle East to get the detail just right for his best-known, and most critically appraised work, *The Finding of the Saviour in the Temple*. Ironically, the cast of Jewish faces you see staring out at you belong not to natives of Palestine, but belong to the artist's East End neighbours – because Hunt could not find any Middle Eastern Jews to sit for him.

Hunt may have died a pillar of the artistic establishment, but 60 years before his demise, he had been the enfant terrible of the English art scene. Along with John Everett Millais and Dante Gabriel Rossetti, he had formed the Pre-Raphaelite Brotherhood and challenged the very idea of what constituted great painting. But, unlike Millais and Rossetti, Hunt wasn't a child of rich parents, and it had been a long, painful slog for him to even become an artist.

Hunt was born in 1827 into a poor family in Cheapside. From his boyhood he was desperate to become a painter. His father, a warehouseman, was having none of it, and the young William was sent to work as a clerk in the City at the age of 12. Hunt practised painting in his spare hours, and in 1844, at the third attempt, he was accepted as a probationer at the Royal Academy School.

William Holman Hunt

Hunt met Millais and Rossetti at the school and introduced the pair to the writings of John Ruskin, the art critic, who was railing against the lush, painterly canvases of the likes of Reynolds, Turner and Constable. Ruskin urged artists to return to the purity, simplicity and accuracy of medieval painting as it was before the painter Raphael.

The group dubbed themselves the Pre-Raphaelite Brotherhood and set about transforming Ruskin's theories into paintings. For Hunt, the painstaking rules they had set themselves meant that his works often took years to complete, as he painted in every blade of grass, every leaf on a tree. Works such as *The Awakening Conscience* and *The Light of the World* took between five and ten years to complete.

He may have been successful, but his painfully slow pace of working meant he wasn't yet rich. So Hunt followed many artists into taking a studio in the East End: space and models for his painstaking portraits were much cheaper east of the City. And like his Pre-Raphaelite brothers,

> "The ideal models were his Jewish immigrant neighbours"

Hunt soon succumbed to a weakness for his beautiful models. But being a religious and high-minded man, Hunt decided to reform and marry East End girl Annie Miller. Both projects ended in failure.

In 1854, Hunt decided to take a trip to the Middle East. His plan was to get as close to the source of the Scriptures as he could, and make his religious work as accurate and detailed as possible. Hunt gleaned a huge amount of detail of buildings, scenery and vegetation, and excitedly began his masterwork. But try as he might, he could find no local people who were prepared to sit for him. Disconsolate, he returned to his East End studio, where *Saviour* sat unfinished for six more years. In 1860, Hunt realised the answer had been staring him in the face. The Jewish immigrants of the East End had the profiles and features he needed.

Designers, Painters and Photographers

The barman and the painter

The death of John Edwards, barman, photographer, dyslexic illiterate, and multi-millionaire, severed one of the last ties between the East End and post-war Soho. It was a time that saw millionaire painters such as Francis Bacon and Lucien Freud rub shoulders with journalists such as Daniel Farson, Graham Mason and Jeffrey Bernard; and with East Enders like the Kray Brothers, petty crook George Dyer, and Edwards himself.

Edwards' last days, as a millionaire ex-pat, sipping pink champagne at Le Cafe Royale in Pattaya, Thailand, were a long way from his East End roots. Born one of six children to a family of dockers turned publicans, his inability to read was no barrier to work in the family pubs. The chain of events that led to him becoming Francis Bacon's friend, minder and muse began one day in 1974 at one of the pubs, the Swan, where John worked for his brother, later to become a successful businessman.

Muriel Belcher, owner of infamous Soho club The Colony Room, used to come to the East End to meet her friend, Joan Littlewood, driving force between the Theatre Royal, Stratford. Belcher told Edwards to order up some champagne, as she would be visiting with Littlewood and Bacon. The group never showed, and a furious John descended on the Dean Street club, to berate Bacon for lumbering him with an unsaleable bottle of bubbly.

Bacon might have been Britain's most famous and expensive

John Edwards and Francis Bacon

painter, but he wasn't deterred or offended by Edwards' directness. Art critic Richard Cork described the Colony Room of the time as 'a mixture of Soho bohemians, often with plummy public school accents, and an East End contingent, with broken noses, looking thuggish, but quite often gay ... the whole mixture which fascinated Francis'. Bacon had been a regular at the Colony since its opening in 1948, entertaining the mixed company with his spiky, cruel wit. The artist immediately offered to buy Edwards dinner at Wheeler's in Old Compton Street – favourite hangout of the Colony crew. The surprised barman ordered caviar and the two became immediate friends.

They may have seemed an unlikely couple: Edwards was 22, Bacon 41 years older, both were gay, though they maintained that their friendship was platonic. But John's lack of reverence for Bacon, initially knowing nothing of his art, was refreshing for a man who, though his paintings sold for millions, did his work in a squalid studio/flat, lit by bare bulbs and strewn with rubbish.

It was a sometimes chaotic life: Bacon had met his longtime lover and subject George Dyer when he caught the East End crook attempting to burgle his flat in 1964. The two were together for eight turbulent years before Dyer died, overdosing on a cocktail of alcohol and drugs on the eve of one of Bacon's shows. But though Bacon and his friends consumed enormous amounts of booze, there was discipline there too: the painter was always at work in his studio at 7am. Over the next years he was to paint many studies of his new friend John.

"The rich artist loved Edwards' lack of reverence"

Bacon died in 1992, leaving the bulk of his estate, nearly £11m, to Edwards. And though the years after were beset by legal wrangles with Bacon's London gallery, the money allowed John to live well. And a year before his death he set up the John Edwards Charitable Foundation, to advance studies of the artist.

Designers, Painters and Photographers

Etching a place in art history

There aren't many artists who enjoy success in both Fine and Commercial Art. But William Larkins' draughtsmanship made him as comfortable designing the Black Magic box as producing exquisite etchings of his native East End.

He was born in 1901 into a Bow family of steeplejacks. It was a family skill that came into its own when he began studying at Goldsmiths College of Art. His fellow students were stunned by his contribution to a student rag – climbing Nelson's Column to give it a clean! One of those students was Graham Sutherland, later to become one of the greatest English painters of the twentieth century. But during his time at Goldsmiths he was consumed by producing etchings – inspired in part by Larkins' work.

'I knew William Larkins very well,' he remembered years later. 'As students we sat side by side, he a little earlier than I in arriving at the School of Art, often as early as 6.30 in the morning, while I arrived about 7.00.' Sutherland describes Larkins etchings as 'exceptional – very small but packed with insight. He managed to combine a highly complex technique with an air of simplicity'. Larkins introduced his fellows to the work of great 19th century artist and etcher Samuel Palmer.

Much of the vitality and detail of Larkins' early work derived from the fact he was drawing on his East End childhood. With his detailed local knowledge he was plundering an area rich in character and street theatre for his pictures. A boot stall in

William Larkins

Whitechapel; a brewery and timber yard in Mile End; an Aldgate tripe dresser's shop; the rays of sunlight beaming down into Whitechapel Underground Station. Mundane street scenes became chiaroscuro triumphs.

It was an extraordinary burst of creativity. But though he travelled, making etchings of Bruges, Paris, New York, as well as idyllic scenes from the Welsh countryside, most of the work would be compressed into a few years of the 1920s. Etching had been a lucrative business in the early years of the century – with prints sold in editions of thousands. But as the 1920s wore on, it lost out to photography. The Depression of the late 20s sounded the final death knell for the labour intensive and thus expensive business of etchings. And so, although in 1925 he had been exhibited at the Los Angeles Museum, by the 1930s William was looking for a solid career.

In 1932, Larkins joined giant advertising agency J Walter Thompson as an art director. He soon became an ad man as much as an artist, getting involved in selling and marketing. Back at the drawing board, he produced the famed Black Magic chocolates box (a design that for 35 years was largely unchanged). He came up with the wrapper for Aero and designed the Lux soap flakes box. Then, in 1940 he formed the Larkins Studio, which went on to produce films and animations on tank and aircraft recognition for the Ministries of Defence and Information, as well as making propaganda and independent cartoons – entertainment and a boost to the war effort.

"Most of his best work was done before he hit 25"

Larkins spent the last 30 years of his life as art director of *Reader's Digest*. With his jack-of-all-trades approach taking in sales, promotion and advertising, it was a million miles from his early days at Goldsmiths. In later life he was dismissive of his work of the 1920s – yet in his stark pictures there is captured all the vibrancy of the East End streets.

Designers, Painters and Photographers

CR Ashbee's rustic dream

In our modern age, when specialisation is everything, CR Ashbee would be a man out of time. Architect, town planner, silversmith and furniture designer, he created fine Chelsea townhouses and restored artisans cottages, published fine editions of Erasmus and prayer books, and designed colourful necklaces modelled on Renaissance jewellery. But central to all his work was his vocation as a social reformer. .

Charles Robert Ashbee was born in London, the son of a wealthy City merchant. As a young man he lived at the pioneering Toynbee Hall settlement in Whitechapel where he started classes in art and craft. These gave birth to first the School of Handicraft in 1887, and then the Guild of Handicraft in 1888.

Ashbee's work was fired by his adherence to the Arts and Crafts Movement which flourished in Victorian Britain. The movement, with its figureheads William Morris and John Ruskin, was a revolt against industrialisation and its dehumanizing effect on the artisan classes. It was based on simple designs and the use of nature as a template for the patterns used in jewellery, architecture, fabric design and the rest.

The movement had crystallised when a group of young London architects formed the Art Workers' Guild in 1884 – their dream was to break down barriers between architects, artists, designers and makers. Bright colours, rich textures and elaborate patterns featured, but sometimes the work was very plain – shockingly so

CR Ashbee

to the Victorian critic, used to high decoration. One reviewer in 1899 referred to one piece as looking 'like the work of a savage'.

It was a holistic movement, embracing music and drama. Composers such as Vaughan Williams and Holst shared the movement's love of the countryside and folk traditions. As part of the movement, Arnold Dolmetch pioneered the revival of early English music while Cecil Sharp and others collected traditional folk songs and dances. Playwright and author Bernard Shaw and poet John Masefield were enthusiastic followers.

By the turn of the century, Ashbee had a successful business in the Mile End Road, but the grime and grind of the East End would never satisfy him. His credo was that 'in a modern industrialised society every person must be an artist or be reduced to a mechanical drudge'.

Ashbee was convinced the future of the Guild lay in the country, and in summer 1902 The Guild of Handicraft moved to the Cotswold wool town of Chipping Campden. Not only did the works go, so did the workforce, and the influx of 70 cockney craftsmen and their families had a major impact on the town's population of only 1500.

> "He moved the firm from Mile End to the Cotswolds. Workers were now owners"

From being bonded employees, the workers now had a stake in the company, but the finances were shaky and the venture folded in 1907. But that wasn't the end of the Cotswold cockneys. Many had a taste for business and the guild became an association of small shops, with men like Alec Miller, Jim Pyment, Will and George Hart turning out fine work. To this day, Hart Silversmith's is run by George's grandson David. And Ashbee's dream was hugely influential. The guild, with its romantic attempt to reconstruct society inspired groups in Britain, America, South Africa and Europe.

Designers, Painters and Photographers

Graphic image of post-War age

Some of the most memorable graphic images of mid-twentieth century Britain were the work of Whitechapel artist and designer Abram Games. And as a poster designer in World War II his skills, his love for his country and his horror at what was happening to fellow Jews in Europe, came together to create some of the most powerful poster art this country has seen.

Games was born in 1914 in Whitechapel. By 1930, the family name had been Anglicised to 'Games' and Abram had left Hackney Downs School, enrolling as a paying student at St Martin's School of Art. He lasted just two terms. Disillusioned with the style and quality of tuition he quit. It was an early show of Abram's determination and focus – and a rock-solid certainty that he knew best.

For the next two years he worked in his father's photographic studio. All the while he was attending evening classes in life drawing, and studying anatomy in his spare time, making regular visits to the Royal College of Surgeons. Working so closely with photo-processing he became fascinated by the increased use of photography in poster and iconic art. He was an admirer of Man Ray and the photo-montage pioneer John Hearfield. But as he distilled his hundreds of hours of painstaking practice into his own style, it wasn't a camera he picked up to make his images, but the airbrush. His economy of style and execution was suited to poster art, where a powerful image had to be swiftly conveyed

Abram Games

– from the side of a bus or the window of an underground train. But Games's next job, as a studio boy with London commercial art studio Askew-Younge, was shortlived. He was fired in 1936 for a 'rebellious and undisciplined attitude'.

His conscription into the infantry in 1940 was the turning point. Games was a willing soldier. He had two reasons to fight, as he said later: 'I loved my country ... and there was what was happening to the Jews in Germany.' But his great contribution wasn't with a rifle. Troubled by the lack of information on health and hygiene in army barracks, Abram wrote an anonymous memo to the War Office, recommending instructional posters.

The War Office took up the challenge, handing Games the job. Between 1941 and 1945 he produced 100 posters – warning of the dangers of careless talk, unwashed feet, unbrushed teeth and unprotected sex. His series of posters with Frank Newbould, *Your Britain, fight for it now*, created from 1942, showed the gleaming, light-filled architecture of the new Britain rising from the rubble of the Blitz.

> "Churchill demanded the removal of one poster as falsely optimistic"

They were beguiling and optimistic images, though the reality couldn't always match the dream. Prime Minister Winston Churchill demanded the withdrawal of one, showing the new Finsbury Health Centre as a shining white palace of concrete and glass. The Prime Minister called it 'exaggerated and distorted propaganda. The soldiers know their homes are not like that'.

Games charted a fast-changing post-War Britain. Among hundreds of briefs were designs for the Festival of Britain, tourist posters for London, and a Freedom from Hunger poster for the UN. While producing work for clients like BOAC and Gestetner he would give up weekends to support voluntary agencies supporting Jewish refugees. Games died in 1996.

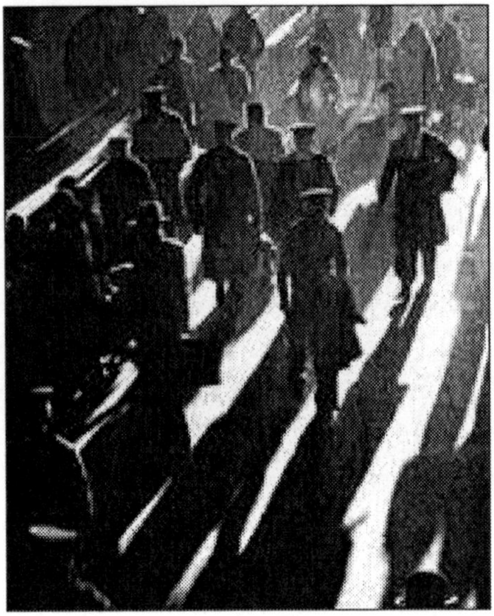

Philanthropists, benefactors and abolitionists

Granville Sharp 206; Hannah Billig 208; Angela Burdett-Coutts 210; Tubby Clayton 212; George Peabody 214.

Philanthropist, Benefactors and Abolitionists

The unlikely abolitionist

Nothing in Granville Sharp's background would have suggested that he was to become one of England's most celebrated campaigners for the abolition of slavery. Yet a chance encounter in Wapping turned the course of his life forever, and hastened the demise of that evil trade.

Sharp was born in Durham on November 10, 1735. One of eight children, he was also the youngest son, and missed out on the formal education his older brothers enjoyed. Instead he was sent to London, to work in the Spitalfields' linen trade. But though he didn't get the schooling of his professional brothers, he was learning in other ways. He moved from employer to employer, picking up wisdom from each. 'This extraordinary experience has taught me to make a proper distinction between the opinions of men and their persons,' he would write later. Sharp was lodging with his brother, a surgeon in Wapping. One day a black slave, Jonathan Strong, staggered into the house. He had been so badly pistol whipped by his master he was at the point of death.

An appalled Sharp took Strong to St Bartholomew's Hospital, where he lay a full four months recovering from his terrible injuries. Strong related his story – how his owner, David Lisle, had brought him from Barbados, but become unhappy with his work, beaten him and hurled him onto the street. Strong recovered, and the unrepentant Lisle hired two thugs to recapture him. A furious Sharp decided to take up Strong's case, and adopted the role of barrister, arguing that as Jonathan lived in England he was no longer legally a slave.

Many of the judiciary in England were uncomfortable with the slave trade, but it took three years before English law took its course – Strong was freed in 1768. Sharp used the publicity to step up the fight to free all slaves. His argument was that a slave treading on English soil was subject to English law. English law precluded slavery, so 'as soon as any slave sets foot on English territory, he becomes free'. His most famous case came when he represented James Somerset. In what was to become known as the 'Somerset ruling' Sharp won a battle which allowed Somerset to stay in England.

The irony was that Sharp had had to accept the legal existence of slavery in other countries, using it as a tactic to fight slavery in England. The biggest fight was still to come. In 1787, Sharp and his friend Thomas Clarkson formed the Society for the Abolition of the Slave Trade, along with influential Quakers such as John Wesley and Josiah Wedgwood. Their breakthrough came when they persuaded William Wilberforce, the MP for Hull, to be their spokesman in the House of Commons.

"He never saw the abolition of slavery but set it in motion"

Sharp's fight for freedom was taken to other areas too. He sympathised strongly with the revolting American colonists, fought for Parliamentary reform in Britain, propounded the legislative independence of Ireland, and argued against the Navy's use of the pressgang. Things were changing slowly but surely. After the passing of the Abolition of the Slave Trade Act in 1807 Sharp joined Thomas Clarkson and Thomas Fowell Buxton to form the Society for the Mitigation and Gradual Abolition of Slavery. Sadly he would never see abolition come to pass. The great campaigner died on July 6, 1813.

Philanthropist, Benefactors and Abolitionists

The Angel of Cable Street

The life of Hannah Billig was an extraordinary story that took her from Russia to Calcutta and Israel – with a lifetime's dedication to the people of the East End. The story started with Barnet and Millie Billig, Jewish refugees from persecution in Russia, who settled in the Jewish community around Brick Lane.

Barnet worked all hours as a newsagent and then hand-making cigarettes and cigars, while Millie slaved over the cooking, cleaning and washing for her husband and six children. And the kids had to work hard too. There was no playing in the streets like the other children of the neighbourhood, Hannah and her siblings were encouraged to sit and diligently study in their library-like front room.

The Billig parents got their reward when four of the youngsters became doctors, an especial achievement for Hannah in the 1920s when women were expected to marry and keep house. But her ambitions didn't end with qualifying as a doctor, Hannah wanted to put something back into the community that had raised her. Her chance came with a job at the Jewish Maternity Hospital in Whitechapel's Underwood Street.

Billig then set up her own practice in Watney Street. She still lived with her parents in Burdett Road and, by word of mouth, she soon had a flood of patients from all over Wapping and Stepney. With no NHS you had to pay for your treatment in those

Hannah Billig

days. Many poor simply didn't bother to see the doctor – but Hannah would never turn the sick away, following her father by working endless hours. And like her father too, Hannah would encourage the children she saw, telling them to bring along their books so she could read aloud to them.

As war drew on even the Blitz couldn't stop Hannah and her work, as she darted around, tending the sick, as the bombs were dropping around her. On 13 March 1941 she was helping the injured at a blast in Orient Wharf, Wapping. Suddenly there was an explosion and Hannah was blown down the shelter steps. Picking herself up and shaking off the dust she bandaged up her sore ankle and set about pulling others out of the rubble.

After four hours toil she finally took a break, to discover that her own ankle was broken. For her bravery Billig won the George Medal, the civilian's equivalent of the Victoria Cross: the Angel of Cable Street had been born.

In 1942 the Angel spread her wings, signing up for the Indian Army Medical Corps as a Captain and tending the sick and wounded soldiers in Assam, as they retreated from the terrible battles in the jungles of Burma. Malaria and typhus were two of the new diseases Hannah had to contend with and there was worse to come. In 1944 a grain shortage forced thousands of starving peasants into Calcutta in desperate search of food.

> "After four hours she took a break and found her ankle was broken"

Back in Cable Street the good work continued until she decided to retire, in 1964, to Israel. Parties and dinners were held all over the East End in her honour. The restless Hannah soon started work again in the Arab villages and Jewish settlements around her new home in Caesarea and for 20 more years worked tirelessly for new patients and friends. In 1987, aged 86, she died peacefully, having made as much of a mark in her new home as in Cable Street.

Philanthropist, Benefactors and Abolitionists

A banker with a conscience

When Coutts moved into Canary Wharf Tower, the posh people's bank was simply renewing its aquaintance with the East End. For, a century ago, one of their number was spreading the family cash in a different fashion – by helping the Tower Hamlets poor.

Angela Burdett-Coutts had everything going for her and no need to lift a finger. In 1837, at the age of just 23 she inherited a vast fortune from grandfather Thomas Coutts, the banker, and promptly became one of the world's richest women and the object of many keen suitors.

The Victorian era in England is infamous for the obscene gap between the hugely wealthy and the desperately poor. But while there were many exploitative factory owners or businessmen there were others working as philanthropists, desperately trying to improve the lot of the working man, woman and child. Angela ignored the offers of marriage and the comfortable life that awaited her and threw herself into her religious faith and using her cash to fight for social reform and education for the poor. She didn't turn her back on the family firm though. With amazing energy she not only threw herself into setting up charities, projects for housing the poor, childcare schemes, fighting for work for women – she also took a keen interest in the running of Coutts Bank, becoming a sharp businesswoman and a key part of the family firm.

Angela Burdett-Coutts

The East End of the nineteenth century may have been the hub of the British Empire's trade but many of its people lived in terrible poverty. Coutts set about making things better. She supplied funds to build the church of St John's in Vincent Street, Limehouse, later to become Halley Street. She set up a sewing school in Brown's Lane, Spitalfields and women came to learn sewing skills.

Many East End women were driven into prostitution by poverty. Charles Dickens became a firm friend of Angela and helped her to set up a house of rescue for young prostitutes. He later marked her philanthropic works for Londoners by dedicating his novel, *Martin Chuzzlewit*, to Coutts.

Not all of her work was so successful. A big problem for working people was getting affordable fresh food, vital for their good health apart from anything else. But London markets had to pay tolls, which racked up the price of the goods on sale. Angela took a radical approachl: £20,000 of her own cash paid for the building of the Columbia Market, in Bethnal Green. The new venue had room for 400 stalls but the market never made money. Various schemes were tried, including a go at running it as a fish market, but in 1886 the redoubtable founder at last admitted defeat and the market shut down.

> "Not all her work was a success. Columbia Market never made money"

A revolutionary figure, Angela was recognised for her energy and works. She was the first female 'freeman' of the City and the first woman made a peer in her own right. When Baroness Burdett-Coutts died in 1906 she had left a lasting mark on the East End, with huge schemes like the building of model tenements in Columbia Square, Bethnal Green, and with her name – which lives on in the shape of Angela Street, Baroness Road and Burdett Road.

Philanthropist, Benefactors and Abolitionists

The man who lit the Toc H lamp

As dim as a Toc H lamp, went the joke. But for World War One soldiers and generations of young people since, the Toc H club, founded by local vicar Philip Clayton, was a beacon of hope.

Philip Thomas Byard Clayton was born in Queensland, Australia, on 12 December, 1885 to English ex-patriates. Two years later, Philip and his parents returned to England, where he attended St Paul's School. He then went on to Exeter College, Oxford, where he studied theology, coming down with a first class degree.

The newly graduated Philip – or Tubby as he became known – entered the church, and in 1910 went as a curate to St Mary's Portsea. Soon his life was overtaken by the Great War and, in 1915, he went to France as an army chaplain. It was during the war that his real life's work began. In December 1915, he opened Talbot House in Poperinge, a club lying just behind the lines in Flanders, which saw some of the worst of the fighting. It became known to the thousands of soldiers who found a touch of home there and a brief respite from the horrors of war as 'Toc H'. This was a reference to the army signallers' code, whereby the initials of Talbot House – TH – would become Toc H.

During the war, hundreds of men committed themselves, should they survive, to entering the church as priests. Tubby's first task after the war was at the Ordination Test School, estab-

Tubby Clayton and Toc H

lished in a disused gaol in Knutsford, Cheshire, where these men were prepared for theological college. He was the main inspiration and was, for a short time, a member of the teaching staff. Already, however, he was planning for the rebirth of Toc H.

This was not to be a simple ex-service organisation, but an attempt to preserve and hand on to succeeding generations the special atmosphere and camaraderie which had characterised Talbot House in Poperinge. It was an ambitious project, but Tubby was determined to carry Toc H into Civvy Street.

In 1922, with the Toc H movement still in its infancy, he was asked by Archbishop Davidson to become the vicar of All Hallows by the Tower, in Newark Street, E1, and to bring new life to an ancient church with an uninterested and dwindling congregation.

He was the vicar of All Hallows for the next 40 years and Tower Hill was his home for the rest of his life. He travelled the world, renewing wartime friendships and launching Toc H throughout what was then the Empire. But Tower Hill was not neglected. He began formulating and discussing plans to beautify the area and to create open space. His tireless efforts saw the birth in 1932 of the Tower Hill Improvement Trust. In 1940, All Hallows Church was bombed and Tubby's first post-war priority was its rebuilding – a task which required all his energy and powers of persuasion. He succeeded, of course. In 1962, Tubby resigned as vicar of the newly rebuilt All Hallows. He remained in Tower Hill, active in both Toc H and the Winant and Clayton Volunteers, until his death, just after his 87th birthday, in 1972.

"Toc H was a bold bid to carry wartime camaraderie into peace"

Today, Toc H is as active as ever. Volunteers work on community projects, such as children's playschemes, conservation or construction projects, the running of leadership training courses and first aid training.

Philanthropist, Benefactors and Abolitionists

Shocked into philanthropy

George Peabody grew up on the other side of the world from the East End. And as he left school at 11, going to work to help support his seven siblings, it was unlikely that he learned much about London in the classroom either. But the poverty of the East End was to strike a chord with this extraordinary figure.

Peabody was born in Danvers, Massachusetts in 1795, and had already been a working man for seven years when he signed up as a volunteer in the United States' war with Britain in 1812. While serving, he showed the first signs of the financial acumen that was to make his fortune, raising the financial backing to found the wholesale dry goods firm of Peabody, Riggs and Co.

In 1816, Peabody moved to Baltimore and the thriving business established branches in Philadelphia and New York. Seeking wider business opportunities, Peabody travelled to England in 1827 to negotiate the sale of American cotton in Lancashire. In 1837, the year Victoria ascended the throne, he made his home in London. In 1851, Britain staged The Great Exhibition of the World of Industry of All Nations in London. But despite the brave new world promised within the Crystal Palace, England was in social turmoil.

London was paying a terrible price for uncontrolled industrialization and sprawling urban growth. The homeless and destitute were everywhere on East End streets, while Charles Dickens

George Peabody

scourged the heartless industrialists in works including *Hard Times*. It was social reformer Lord Shaftesbury who was the catalyst when the shaken Peabody asked what he could do to alleviate the suffering of his fellow Londoners. 'Low-rent housing', was the politician's reply, and Peabody stumped up the astonishing figure of $2.5 million. The trustees' brief was to use the cash to benefit Londoners, who had to be poor, have moral character and be a good member of society.

And so the first of dozens of Peabody Buildings was raised in the East End. The buildings at 135-153 Commercial Road were for the housing of 40 low-income families, with shops, laundries and baths – undreamed-of luxuries at the time. The buildings still stand but, in a sign of the times, they are now privately owned.

Nobody knows for sure how much the benevolent millionaire gave away, but there are recorded donations of more than $8m, most in his own lifetime.

Peabody died in London on 4 November, 1869. At the request of the Dean of Westminster and with the approval of Queen Victoria, he was given a temporary burial in Westminster Abbey. His will said he should be buried in the town of his birth, Danvers, and the prime minster, William Gladstone, arranged for Peabody's remains to be returned to America on the Monarch, the newest and largest ship in Her Majesty's Navy.

Peabody was honoured on both sides of the Atlantic for his generosity. He was one of only two Americans to have been awarded the Freedom of the City of London (the other was General Dwight D Eisenhower). A statue to George Peabody still stands in the heart of London's financial district. In the United States, he was awarded the Congressional Medal in 1867.

More importantly though, throughout London, the Peabody Trust still provides affordable housing for 26,000 people – George Peabody's legacy goes on into a third century.

> "During his life, Peabody gave away $8m"

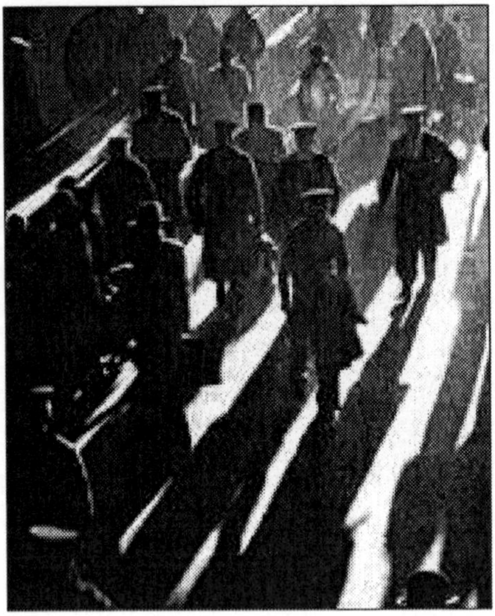

Entrepreneurs, industrialists & business people

Lew Grade 218; William Caslon 220; Thomas Frye 222; William Lusty 224; Sidney Bloom 226; Lesney 228.

Entrepreneurs, industrialists and business people

The man who owned showbiz

Lord Grade was the last great link with the old Jewish East End – the East End of working class lads who transformed themselves through hard work and an eye for the chance into the great entrepreneurs of post-War London.

Louis Winogradsky was born in the Ukrainian town of Tokmak on Christmas Day 1906, to parents Olga and Isaac. But in 1912, along with thousands of other Jewish families, the family fled the pogroms in the Tsar's empire to a new life in the East End. It was an uncertain existence. Within the first months, Isaac had lost all the capital he had brought with him.

While Isaac was making a fresh start managing a cinema in Soho's Brewer Street (the site of the later Paul Raymond Revuebar), young Lou was skipping Saturday morning synagogue to go to the pictures. He didn't find his niche straight away. First he decided to put his maths brain to use as an accountant, then at 15 became an agent for a rag trade firm. The budding entrepreneur soon set up his own firm with his dad, turning out clothes 24 hours a day.

But his energy wasn't confined to work. He loved to go dancing at the East Ham Palais. And in 1926, 'Louis Grad' was crowned World Solo Charleston Champion at the Albert Hall. The judge? No less than Fred Astaire. Lew was hooked and sold up the firm to become a professional dancer, 'the man with the musical feet'. By now he was 'Lew Grade', after his name was

Lew Grade

misspelt on a bill, but by the 1930s knee problems – and the fact that the Charleston had had its day – prompted him to move into management. He first worked for the agent Joe Collins, Joan and Jackie's dad. Then, after returning from a wartime stint in the Army, set up with his brother Leslie. As a minnow in a hard business, Lou had to fight for his share, and he went to the States to snatch up-and-coming acts, bringing Lena Horne, Johnny Ray and Jack Benny to London.

The biggest agent in Britain now moved into fledgling commercial TV. The Midlands franchise (ATV, now Central) was a flop at first. But Lou knew what sold, and *Crossroads*, *Emergency Ward 10*, *General Hospital* and *The Muppet Show* made the station one of the giants, along with Granada and Thames.

> "The last impresario to leap from music hall to TV and movies"

Films beckoned too with successes like the *Pink Panther* series and *On Golden Pond*. And Lew got there nearly 20 years before James Cameron and Leonardo Di Caprio, though his 1980 production *Raise The Titanic* was such a flop that he remarked that 'it would have been cheaper to lower the Atlantic.' Joking apart, the financial disaster nearly sunk Grade's company ACC, and it signalled the beginning of the end of his one-man operation.

But even when he'd loosened the reins at ACC, Lew just wasn't able to stop working – finding new talent and setting up deals well into his nineties. Even the energetic Grade couldn't finish one of his projects though – he had bought 450 of Barbara Cartland's books with the aim of making films of them ... all of them. A lucky escape perhaps.

One of the big men of the entertainment industry, he'll always be remembered for his chutzpah and big cigar. Louis Winogradsky died Baron Grade of Elstree, just days short of his 92nd birthday, Christmas Day.

Entrepreneurs, industrialists and business people

Man with his work cut out

When William Caslon set up shop in the Minories in 1716, he had his work, and his future, cut out. The young Caslon, who had been born in Cradley, Worcestershire in 1692, was a skilled engraver and toolmaker. He made a living engraving Government marks on the locks of guns, and also turned his cutting skills to punch-cutting, making the hard metal punches used to make the moulds for type founding. The type-makers would then flow molten lead into Caslon's moulds, to produce a single piece of type, ready for typesetting.

But London typesetters were held in low regard. English printing was behind its Continental counterparts, and most of the typefaces used in London presses came from Dutch typefounders. All this was to change in 1719, when a group of London printers and booksellers asked the young engraver to cut a font of 'Arabic' type, for a new Psalter and New Testament. Copies of this were to accompany the missionaries aboard the vessels flooding out of Wapping, on the trade routes to the Far East. The evangelistic bookmen hoped that they would be able to export Christianity about the merchant ships.

Dissatisfied with the dull Dutch typefaces on offer, Caslon soon took to cutting his own font designs. He began with the Dutch faces as his model, but refined them, making them more delicate and inventive. An excited Caslon went on to create a large number of 'exotic' typefaces.

William Caslon

Having added design to his punch-cutting skills, the enterprising Caslon soon realised that there was a business in the making. Craftsman, artist and businessman in one, he became the first great English type-founder. He set up his foundry in Chiswell Street, in the City, in 1720, and built a country home in rural Bethnal Green.

The taste for Caslon spread to the United States, and Caslon was the typeface used for the Declaration of Independence in 1776, joining that other great export from the East End - the Liberty Bell. The family business, meanwhile, had passed from father to son, through four generations, all of them called, with a remarkable lack of imagination for such a creative dynasy, William Caslon.

But typefaces, like any other design, go in and out of fashion, and by the early 1800s, the taste for Caslon had dropped off, in favour of newer typefaces, and in 1819, William Caslon IV sold the Chiswell Street business to a firm of Sheffield typefounders named Stephenson Blake and Co.

"Caslon's new typeface graced the United States Declaration of Independence"

But around 1840, there was a revival of interest in the fonts. This was a burgeoning time for English print, with presses becoming more plentiful, printing cheaper, and an explosion in the number of pamphlets, newspapers, and cheap popular novels. Printers found that the Caslon faces, which were unfailingly elegant, clear and easy on the eye, worked as well as they ever had, and better than most. George Bernard Shaw, went so far as to insist Caslon be the only typeface used in his books.

The Caslon connection with typefounding disappeared for good when the other family foundry, HW Caslon & Co, having passed down through various members of the family until 1937, was itself sold to Stephenson Blake.

Entrepreneurs, industrialists and business people

The East End Wedgewood

Wedgewood, Meissen, Delft – all are world famous names in the world of pottery. But 250 years ago it was Bow pottery that was drawing the eyes of the world, and all thanks to a young Irish painter who settled in the East End. Thomas Frye was born in Dublin in 1710 and, having won acclaim in his native Ireland as a painter,came to London in 1734. One of his first coups as a portraitist was his commission to paint the Prince of Wales, for the Saddlers' Company. Among the other specialities of the multi-talented artist were miniature painting, mezzotint, engraving and enamel work.

But Frye was also a keen inventor and his love of art and love of discovery came together when he devised a method of producing porcelain, the beautiful translucent china pottery as popular in the eighteenth century as it is today. Porcelain may have been popular at the time but there were two big problems. First it was very fragile and second, with all the pieces coming from abroad, it was very expensive. Frye had a solution. As a result of his experiments with china clay he discovered a method of making porcelain out of bone ash. This produced a porcelain of brilliant whiteness and luminescence and extraordinary durability.

The second solution was obvious – he would set up a factory in London to manufacture his new china. In 1744, Frye and his partner, Edward Heylen took out a patent for the production of artificial soft-paste porcelain. The inventors and manufacturers of

Thomas Frye

porcelain in England called their product 'New Canton', a nod to the pottery from the Far East with which they hoped to compete.

The next step was to set up a factory. Frye had attracted the interest of the rich and powerful Peers family. They owned huge tracts of land across Bromley, Bow and Stratford. They were also directors of the all-powerful East India Company, mainstay of Britain's overseas trade at the time, and whose great ships unloaded their imported wares on the Isle of Dogs, near the mouth of Bow Creek.

The Court Book of 1744 shows Edward Heylen acquired a property on the London side of the River Lea, at Bow. And, with the backing of the Peers family, the china factory was set up near Bow Bridge in 1749. The Bow Porcelain Manufactory of New Canton was ready to start work.

Frye's work was down to earth from the word go, concentrating on 'the more ordinary sorts of ware for common use'. That didn't please the purists. One expert has described Bow porcelain as 'a peasant art which appeals to an unacademic sense of beauty rather than taste.' Still, what do experts know. Very soon the demand was so great that another factory was opened, this time on the Stratford side of the River Lea. But despite his success Frye was still toiling long hours in the factory furnaces as well as designing new lines. Eventually the long hours took their toll. Frye died in 1762, at the age of just 52, and is buried in Hornsey Churchyard.

"Meissen, Delft and Wedgewood ... add Bow to the list"

The work went on, but without his driving force and energy, quality slipped. Their was another 13 years of production at Bow, but towards the end products were underfired and lacked their earlier translucence and in 1776 the works closed. Frye's legacy remains. His processes changed pottery forever and one of his daughters went on to work for Wedgewood. And you still find Bow porcelain today – tough enough to last 250 years.

Entrepreneurs, industrialists and business people

Bromley's wicker man

The East End has a long tradition in furniture-making – with one-man workshops of cabinet makers and upholsterers peppering Shoreditch and Spitalfields during the 19th and early 20th centuries. But the greatest success story came about in a most unexpected way: the combination of the inventive genius of a young American and the entrepreneurial eye of a Bow businessman.

William Lusty started his business in 1872 out of a hardware shop in Bromley-by-Bow. William was a jack of all trades – salvaging driftwood fallen from barges out of the canals, and fashioning the lumber into packing crates. By the new century, Lusty's was a thriving business. During World War I, the business boomed, opening up new production lines to make munitions cases. Peacetime meant idle assembly lines and a huge factory to keep busy. So when a New York agent for the packing case business telegrammed details of a new invention to William, he jumped at the opportunity. Marshall Burns Lloyd had been born in Minnesota in 1858, the son of an English immigrant. Lloyd typified the adventurous spirit of the new Americans, travelling the country, working as an insurance salesman, a property speculator and an inventor.

He had noticed the elaborate – and expensive – wicker furniture popular with style-conscious Americans. It was all handwoven, and having attempted to apply the new principles of

Feature title

mechanisation and line production, Marshall figured wicker furniture could only be made by hand. Instead, he used the new skill of twisting paper to make fake wicker, crucially adding his own idea – a core of steel wire to strengthen the weave, making it strong enough to use as furniture. Lloyd Loom furniture became a sensation in America. Classy tables, chairs and bureaux became affordable to ordinary Americans through mail-order catalogues.

Lusty's would corner the British market, Lloyd the American, and designers from both companies would pool knowledge and ideas. But the British proved less keen than the Americans. The Brits insisted on seeing Lloyd Loom as garden furniture, and given the vagaries of the English summer, there was a limited demand for it. By the mid-1920s, Lusty's was on the verge of collapse.

Its fortunes were changed by an inspired advertising campaign. 'Bring our furniture into the home', ran the copyline, and people began to do just that. Sales picked up and, when LNER decided to furnish its enormous railway hotels with the newly stylish Lloyd Loom pieces, Lusty's had their business made.

> "The chairs could now be seen on ocean liners, in hotels and tea rooms"

The company grew from strength to strength as Lloyd Loom furniture became increasingly popular. It could be seen on ocean liners, in hotels and tea rooms; it became the standard issue for the British Army and RAF all over the world.

But if the First World War had seen a boom in the Lusty factory, it was World War II that was to abruptly end things. Standing right by the East India Docks, on the afternoon of September 7, 1940, the factory was destroyed by firebombs. Fortunately, it was a Saturday and the workforce were at home. Lusty's moved to Martley, Worcestershire, in 1963. But flip one of the older chairs over and you will see the distinctive Lusty label, bearing the address Bromley-by-Bow E3.

Entrepreneurs, industrialists and business people

Blooms went off the menu

For many, Bloom's Restaurant was symbolic of the Jewish East End. When The Whitechapel eaterie went, in 1996, it was a sad sign of how the Jewish population of Tower Hamlets had declined and dispersed. For others, Bloom's was a good place to eat, an experience sharpened by some of the most spectacularly rude service in London. The man responsible for rise of Bloom's was Sidney Bloom, who died in 2003, aged 82. In 1952 he established the East End establishment which became 'Britain's most famous kosher restaurant' (as it boldly claimed above the front door).

The original Bloom's had been established by Sidney's father, Morris, a Lithuanian immigrant who arrived in London in 1912. He set up the first restaurant in Brick Lane in 1920. During the early 1930s, the restaurant moved to the corner of Old Montague Street and, in 1952, to Whitechapel High Street.

The 1950s East End was the centre of London's Jewish community, and the reopened Bloom's was an instant success with both local people and celebrities. Everybody would queue for their lockshen or gefilte fish – even Charlie Chaplin. The great London comic was a friend of Bloom, but when the restaurateur invited him to jump the queue, the modest Chaplin declined and waited his turn. Other celebs were less accommodating. Frank Sinatra ordered a special delivery from Bloom's to his suite at the Savoy. Sidney obliged, putting the meal on silver plates. The

Bloom's

food was enjoyed, but the plates were never seen again, to the horror of the parsimonious Bloom. This, after all, was a man who insisted that his waiters buy each meal from the kitchen, the staff then earning commission on what they sold.

This unique system of payment produced Bloom's famous quality of service, politely described as 'informal'. With the waiters on piecework, it was unsurprising that they would bully customers into eating quickly. "From the welcome, 'Sit there and wait till I'm ready,' to the slamming down of the bill, the customer was the enemy," remembered Simon Jenkins in an *Evening Standard* piece.

Yet the food was so good customers would tolerate the rudeness. The noise of people waiting and dining was 'immense. You could stand up and sing an operatic aria without attracting attention,' recalled John Sandilands. The core clientele was now the grandchildren of those who, like Morris Bloom, had travelled from Eastern Europe, from Germany, Slovenia and Lithuania. Among their number were celebrities, like boxer Max Baer, musician Ronnie Scott, actor Steven Berkoff and film producer David Conroy. When Cliff Richard visited Bloom's to dine during the early sixties, the crowd outside grew so large that the restaurant's front window was broken.

"Sinatra ate his meal but enraged Bloom by failing to return the plates"

But by the early nineties the restaurant racked up a half million pound loss, and in 1996 the restaurant was in the newspapers for all the wrong reasons. The food had to be kosher, of course, but the restaurant was found guilty of cutting corners and had its licence withdrawn. A month later Bloom's of Whitechapel closed its doors. East Enders nostalgic for salt beef, gefilte fish and pickled herrings now have to travel to the thriving Golders Green branch to stock up.

Entrepreneurs, industrialists and business people

A motor in a Matchbox

Take a walk north along the River Lea and, just before you hit Hackney Wick, you will see the name 'Lesney' emblazoned on the wall of a decaying blue building. Now the Lesney factory is just another industrial relic, but once it produced the Matchbox cars, trucks, buses and more which enchanted post-War British schoolchildren. And it happened by accident.

Leslie and Rodney Smith were unrelated schoolchums who, in one of those quirks of fate which often spark great events, were reunited during their World War II service in the Royal Navy. Both were engineers and both dreamed of running their own companies once the fighting was over – so they decided they would go into business together.

On 19 June 1947 they sealed their partnership, taking an amalgam of Leslie and Rodney to form Lesney Products – for all their ambitions, the pair had yet to decide what they would be making! With £600 of combined funds, the two bought an old pub, The Rifleman, upriver at Edmonton, and kitted it out with Government surplus die-casting machinery. And, joined by expert die-caster Jack Odell, the company joined the scores of other post-War start-ups, as Britain rebuilt its economy and industry for peacetime.

The company would take on any and every job, subcontracting their skills to the major engineering firms who needed precision die-cast pieces. But, as the Christmas of 1948 approached, orders

Lesney and Matchbox

dropped off, and the Smiths decided to cast around for a way to keep the machines busy and the revenue rolling in. They produced miniatures of the vehicles Britons saw everyday, on thousands of building sites reconstructing the country. A traction engine, cement mixer, tractor and bulldozer were the first off the production line, and Lesney set about selling them to local shops.

Fired by their success, the Smiths decided to pitch the bigger toy stores. They weren't enthusiastic. The tiny cars were described as 'Christmas cracker trash' by one buyer. But children loved them. Lesney, in fact, had difficulty meeting demand and soon 13 Woolworths stores placed orders.

Manufacturing was tough in post-War Britain. From 1950 to 1952, during the Korean War, the Government limited use of zinc to essential purposes, and Lesney made only a tin Jumbo the Elephant toy. But as the 1950s wore on, business took off. The company dumped the bigger toys and concentrated all its manufacturing on miniatures. Rather than an offshoot of the business it became the core, and Lesney went into business with an East End firm

"Dismissed as Christmas cracker trash, the toys are now hugely collectable"

called Moko. The two firms registered the name Matchbox, and concentrated on building the range.

Through the 60s and 70s, exports grew to the US and the Far East, and Matchbox became a worldwide name. But the recession of the early 70s, plus a rash of unsuccessful ventures into dolls and Far East production, took their toll. After huge losses, Lesney was declared bankrupt on 11 June 1992. The brand names were bought, distribution switched to companies in the US, Macau, anywhere but the East End in fact. The irony today is that the 'Christmas cracker trash' is hugely collectable – toys bought 40 years ago with pocket money pennies now change hands for hundreds of pounds.

INDEX

1984, 81
A Christmas Carol, 89
A Kid For Two Farthings, 145
A Passage To India, 55
A Touch of Frost, 62
Abbey Mills Pumping Station, 156
ACC, 219
Albatross, 141
Albion, The, 110
Aldersgate (Barbican), 125
Aldgate, 48, 66, 199
Alice's Adventures in Wonderland, 182
All Hallows by the Tower, Newark St, 213
All Or Nothing, 134
Amador, Pedro, 121
Amazing Grace, 130
Angela St, 211
Animal Farm, 81
Animals, The, 147
Anka, Paul, 143
Apocalypse Now, 74
Armistice Day, 103
Army Game, The, 69
Arnold, Matthew, 84
Arnold, Thomas, 84
Art Workers Guild, 200
Arts and Crafts Movement, 200
Ashbee, CR, 200
Askew-Younge, 203
Astaire, Fred, 218
Atkins, Martin, 150
Attlee, Clement (Clem), 11
ATV (Central Television), 219
Australian test cricket team, 108
Awakening Conscience, The, 194
Bacon, Francis, 196
Baer, Max, 227
Bailey, David, 188
Baldock, Teddy, 121
Baldry, Long John, 140
Baroness Rd, 211
Bart, Lionel (Lionel Begleiter), 70, 134
Bartholomew Fair, 41
Barts Hospital, 71, 206
Basildon, 11
Basketball, 112
Batts family, 97
Bazalgette, Sir Joseph, 155, 156
BBC History Magazine, 119
Be Back Soon, 134
Beatles, The, 143, 189
Beatty, Vice Admiral Sir David, 99
Beaumont, Barber, 190
Belcher, Muriel, 196
Belmont's Sebright Hall, 64
Benny, Jack, 219
Bentham, Jeremy 16
Berg, Jack 'Kid' (Judah Bergman), 52, 120
Berkoff, Steven, 52, 227
Beron, Leon, 46
Bespoke Overcoat, The, 145
Bethnal Green, 61, 79, 84, 120, 125, 126, 146, 158, 180, 183, 211, 221
Beveridge, William, 22
Beverley Hills Cop, 52
Big Bow Mystery, The, 91
Bill, The 62
'Bill Sykes', 89
Billig, Hannah, 208
Birch, Eugenius, 162
Bishop of Stepney, 103
Bishopsgate, 40

Bjork, 151
Black Magic Woman, 141
Black Mate, The, 75
Blackfriars, 166
Blackwall, and Tunnel, 94, 110, 154
Blenheim Palace, 170
Blind Beggar of Bethnal Green, 180
Blithe Spirit, 54
Blitz, 35, 129, 189, 209
Blitz, 70
Bloom, Sidney & Morris, 226
Blooms Restaurant, 226
Bloomsbury Group, The, 192
Bludworth, Lord Mayor of London, 79
Blue Lamp, The, 63
Blue Posts, Limehouse, 184
Blur, 134
Bolan, Marc (Mark Feld), 143
Bolingbroke, Henry St John, 20
Bonham, John, 147
Boundary Estate, 56
Bow, 31, 36, 42, 44, 58, 184, 222
Bow Pottery, 222
Boxing, 52
Boy I Love is up in the Gallery, The, 65
Boyle, Robert, 169
Brasher, Chris, 106
Break of Day in the Trenches, 87
Bresslaw, Bernard, 68
Brick Lane, 56, 90, 208, 226
Bridge Over The River Kwai, 55
Brief Encounter, 54
Briggs, Thomas, 42
Brighton, 179
Brighton Beach Scumbags, 53
British Columbia, 100
Bromley-by-Bow, 103, 156, 223, 224
Broughton, Jack, 118
Brown, Charlie, 184
Brown, James, 135
Browning, Robert, 84
Brunel, Isambard Kingdom, 154
Brunel, Marc, 154
Bunyan, John, 144
Burbage, Richard, 60
Burdett Rd, 208, 211
Burdett-Coutts, Angela, 210
Burmese Days, 81
'Butler, Stan', 67
Buxton, Thomas Fowell, 207
Cable Street, 53, 136, 208
Cambridge Heath Road, 126
Cambridge University, 144, 158
Can, 151
Canada, 100
Canals, 167
Canary Wharf, 210
Canning Town, 66
Caribbean Queen, 148
Carrington, 193
Carrington, Dora, 192
Carroll, Lewis, 182
Carry On films, 68
Cartland, Barbara, 219
Cascarino, Tony, 115
Caslon, William, 220
Castle Howard, 170
Chaplin, Charlie, 226
Charles I, King, 182
Charles II, King, 183
Charrington Brewery, Mile End, 127
Charrington, Fred, 126
Cheapside, 194
Chelmsford gaol, 45

Chelsea Hospital, 170
Chicago, Illinois, 113
Children of the Ghetto, 90
China, People's Republic of, 100
Chipping Camden, 201
Chiswell St, 221
Christ Church, Spitalfields, 138, 171
Church of England/Anglicanism, 9, 124
Churchill, Winston, 18, 23, 46, 203
City of London, 90, 194, 211, 215
Clapton, Eric, 140
Clarkson, Thomas, 207
Clayton, Philip (Tubby), 212
Club Row Market, 53
Coborn Road, 58
Coborn, Charles (Colin McCallum), 58
Cochran, Admiral, 155
Cochrane, Eddy, 142
Cohen, Morris 'Two-Gun', 100
Collins, Joe, Joan and Jackie, 219
Collins, Wilkie, 76
Colony Club, The, 196
Columbia Market, 211
Columbia Records, 143
Come My Soul, Thy Suit Prepare, 131
Comedy of Errors, The, 60
Commercial Road, 66, 184, 215
Commercial Street, 138
Conrad, Joseph (Jozef Teodor Konrad Korzeniowski), 55, 74
Conroy, David, 227
Consider Yourself, 134
Constable, John, 195
Cook, Captain James, 96
Cooper's School, 68
Coriolanus, 53
Cork, Richard, 197
Cornell, George, 181
Cornwell, Jackie, 98
Costermongers, 102
Courtenay, Percy, 65
Coutts Bank, 210
Coutts, Thomas, 210
Coward, Noel, 54, 71
Crab, Roger, 182
Cranmer, Archbishop, 29
Crime, 36-49
Cromwell, Oliver, 79, 182
Cromwell, Thomas, 28
Crooks, Will, 155
Cultural Revolution, 101
Cumberland, Duke of (Butcher), 119
Curtain Theatre, Shoreditch, 61
Czukay, Holger, 151
Daily Express, 145
Daily Herald, 11
Daily Sketch, 34
Davidson, Archbishop, 213
Davis, Miles, 137
Day the Earth Caught Fire, The, 144
Dead Secret, The, 77
Decadence, 53
Deer Hunter, The, 56
'Defiance, The', 159
Delfont, Lord Bernard (Boris Winogradsky), 56
Den, The, 115
Depression (1920s), 199
Derby County, 115
Dickens, Charles ('Boz'), 76, 99, 179, 211, 214
Dillon, Bernard, 65
Dirk Bogarde, 63

INDEX

Disraeli, Benjamin, 157
Dixon of Dock Green, 62
'Dixon, George', 63
DLR (Docklands Light Railway), 185
Docks, 10, 24, 166
Doctor Zhivago, 55
Doggett, Thomas, 117
Doggett's Coat and Badge, 116
Dollond and Aitchison, 160
Dollond, John, 160
Dolmetch, Arnold, 201
Donegan, Lonnie, 143
Donovan, Terence, 188
Don't Treat Me Like a Child, 142
Dorsey, Tommy, 137
Dougal, Samuel, 44
Doughty, Katherine, 176
Down and Out in Paris and London, 81
Drake, Sir Francis, 158
Druce, Joseph, 174
Drunkeness and temperance, 126
Duelling, 190
Duffy, Brian, 188
Duke of Westminster 215
Dyer, George, 197
East, 53
East Ham Palais de Danse, 218
East India Company, 223
East India Dock Road, 66, 111, 184, 225
East London Line, 155
Eastern Athaneum, Beaumont Square, 191
Edge, The, 151
Edinburgh University, 166
Edwards, John, 196
Eisenhower, Dwight D, 215
'Eldorado', 95
Eliot, TS, 87
Elizabeth I, Queen, 94
Elizabeth II, Queen, 191
Ellington, Duke, 137
Emergency Ward 10, 219
English Civil War, 78, 182
Epstein, Jacob, 75
Essays in Criticism, 85
Euclid, 168
Evans, Bill, 137
Evening Standard, 227
Everly Brothers, 143, 146
Expresso Bongo, 144
'A Cup Final, 115
Farson, Daniel, 82
Farson's Guide to the British, 83
Fenchurch Street station, 42
Finding of the Saviour in the Temple, The, 194
Finnegan, Chris, 107
First World War, 11
Fleet Street, 78, 86
Fleetwood Mac, 140
Fleetwood, Mick, 140
Football (soccer), 110, 114
Ford, President Gerald, 113
Frampton, Peter, 135
French, John, 188
Frieake, Teddy, 37
Frye, Thomas, 222
Full Metal Jacket, 74
'Fu-Manchu', 34
Fury, Billy, 142
Games, Abram, 202
Gandhi, Mohadas Karamchard

(Mahatma), 12
Geffrye Museum, 61
Geffrye, Robert, 61
General Hospital, 219
Genesis Cinema, Mile End Road, 58
George IV, King (Prince Regent), 179
George Medal, 209
George VI, King, 191
Gertler, Mark, 192
Getz, Stan, 137
Gilbert, Fred, 59
Gilbert, Sir Humphrey, 94
Gladstone, William Ewart, 215
Glamis Road, 89
GLC/London County Council (LCC), 129, 154
Globe Theatre, 60
Glorious Things of Thee are Spoken, 131
God Rest Ye Merry Gentlemen, 89
Golders Green, 227
Goldsmiths College of Art, 198
Gompers, Samuel, 6, 26
Gompertz, Benjamin, 164
Goodman's Fields Theatre, 139
Grade, Leslie, 57, 219
Grade, Lew (Lord Grade/Louis Winogradsky), 56, 218
Grade, Michael, 57
Graham, George, 115
Granada TV, 219
Grant, Peter, 46
Graves, Caroline, 76
Great Eastern Railway, 10
Great Exhibition, 1851, 214
Great Expectations, 54
Great Fire of London, 78, 168, 171
Great Plague, 79
Great Stink, The, 156
Greek, 53
Green, Peter (Greenbaum), 140
Greenwich Hospital, 170
Greenwich Railway Company, 162
Greenwich Seamen's Hospital, 175
Griffith, DW, 35
Griffiths, John, 164
Guyana, 95
Guy's Hospital, 109
Hackney, 42, 71, 202, 228
Haig, Countess, 103
Hampton Court Palace, 170
Hard Times, 215
Harlem Globetrotters, 112
Harlequin Hermit/Arabian Courtesan, 138
Harlow, 184
Harrison, Audley, 107
Hart, Will and George, 201
Hawkins, Coleman, 136
Hawksmoor, Nicholas, 138, 170
Heart of Darkness, 74
Henry VI, 60
Henry VIII, 28
Heylen, Edward, 222
Hill, Benny, 49
Hill, Billy, 49
Hills, Arnold, 110
Hitler, Adolf, 10, 11, 82
'HMS Chester', 98
'HMS Endeavour', 97
'HMS Porpoise', 175
Holiday Camp, 62
'Holy Club', 124
Holly, Buddy, 134, 146

Holman Hunt, William, 194
Holmes, Sherlock, 35
Holst, Gustav, 201
Holyfield, Evander, 120
Holywell Priory, 61
Homage to Catalonia, 81
Hooke, Robert, 168
Horne, Lena, 219
Hornsey, 223
Hotel Babylon, 53
Houndsditch Murders, 18, 46
Houston, Allan, 113
Hoxton, 61, 64
Hue and Cry, 63
'Huggetts, The', 62
Huguenots, 38, 160
Hurley, Alec, 65
Hyde Park, 90
I'd Do Anything, 134
In Which We Serve, 54
Inspector Morse, 62
Invaders of the Heart, 151
Isle of Dogs, 82, 114, 223
Isle of Wight, 168
Italian Conti Stage School, 134
Itchycoo Park, 135
It's a Bit of a Ruin That Cromwell Knocked About, 65
I've Loved Another Girl Since Then, 59
J Walter Thompson, 199
James I, King, 159
James III (of England, VIII of Scotland), 20
Jazz Singer, The, 56
Jenkins, Simon, 227
Jewish immigration, 90
Jews' Free School, 26
John Beverley (Sid Vicious), 150
John Lydon (Johnny Rotten), 150
John Mayall's Bluesbreakers, 140
Jones, John Paul, 147
Jones, Kenney, 135
Jonson, Ben, 61
Jutland, 99
Kafka, Franz, 52
Keep The Aspidistra Flying, 81
'King Cole' (Bripumyarrimin), 109
King of the Schnorrers, 90
King, BB, 140
Kingsley Hall, Bromley-by-Bow, 12
Kirby's Castle, 181
Kirk, Roland, 137
Korean War, 229
Kossoff, David, 145
Kray Brothers, 107, 181, 189
Krays, The, 53
Kubrick, Stanley, 74
Kvetch, 53
Laindon Farm Colony, 11
Lane, Harriet, 36
Lane, Ronnie, 135
Lansbury, George, 10, 191
Larkins, William, 198
Lawrence of Arabia, 55
Lean, Sir David, 54
Led Zeppelin, 146
Leman Street, 52
Lenin, 19
Lennon and McCartney, 143
Lesney, 228
Lester, Doris and Muriel, 12
Levene, Keith, 150
Levin, Bernard, 145
Lewis, Lennox, 107, 120
Lewis, Ted 'Kid', 52, 121

231

INDEX

Leyton, 98
Liberty Bell, 221
Life of a Greenwich Pensioner, The, 175
Light of the World, The, 194
Lightermen, 116
Limehouse, 34, 102, 162, 174, 184, 211
Lincoln's Inn, 158
Lisle, David, 206
Little White Bull, 70
Littlewood, Joan, 196
Livery companies, 116
Living Doll, 71
Living for Kicks, 83
Lloyd Loom, 225
Lloyd, Marie, 64
Lloyd, Marshall Burns, 224
LNER, 225
Lock Up Your Daughters, 70
London Arena, 113
London Palladium, 142
London Underground (The Tube), 157
Lord Jim, 75
Lord's cricket ground, 108
Los Angeles Museum, 199
Love Really Hurts Without You, 148
Lusty, William, 224
Luther, Martin, 125
Lytton Strachey, Giles, 193
Mackintosh, Cameron, 71
Magri, Charlie, 121
Main Plot, The, 95
Make Me an Offer, 144
Malatesta, Errico, 18
Man Who Broke The Bank at Monte Carlo, The, 58
Manchester Utd, 115
Mankewitz, Wolf, 144
Manor Park, 99, 134
Marching, 87
Marchpane, Eliza (Marquesa de), 178
Marriott, Steve, 134
Martin Chuzzlewit, 211
Martin, John 'Mad', 157
Martley, Worcestershire, 225
Marvin, Hank, 140
Marzipan, 178
Masefield, John, 201
Massive Attack, 151
Matchbox Cars/Lesney, 228
Mayhew, Henry, 41
MCC, 108
McLagan, Ian, 135
McMillan's Magazine, 89
McTaggart, Dick, 107
McVie, John, 141
Meath Gardens, 109
Mechanic's Institute, 163
Meikle, Andrew, 166
Mendeloff, Gershon, 121
Mendoza, Daniel, 120
Merceron, Joseph, 38
Merry Go Round, The, 193
Metamorphosis, 52
Methodism, 124
Metropolitan Board of Works, 154
Metropolitan Commission of Sewers, 157
Mile End, 68, 199
Mill, John Stuart, 17
Millais, Sir John Everett, 194
Miller, Alec. 201
Miller, Annie, 195
Milligan, Spike, 137

Millwall Dock, 114
Millwall, FC, 114
Miss Marple, 53
Modern Musick-Master/Universal
Mons, Battle of , 103
Montford, Simon de, 180
Montgomery, Wes, 137
Moonstone, The, 77
Moravians, 124
Morley, Robert, 146
Morris, William, 200
Morrison, Steinie, 46
Most, Mickie, 147
Motza Kleis (Matzo Balls), 90
Mozart, Wolfgang Amadeus, 179
Muller, Franz, 42
Muppet Show, The, 219
Musician, The, 139
Mussolini, 11
My Brother's Keeper, 63
Mystery of Edwin Drood, The, 89
Napier-Bell, Simon, 147
Napoleonic Wars, 190
Nash, Paul, 192
National Service, 71, 146
Nazis, 25
Nelson, Horatio, 161
Nevinson, CRW, 192
'New Canton', 223
New Cross, 115
New Model Army, 183
New South Wales, 174
New Vaudeville Band, The, 147
New York, 136, 176
New Zealand and Maoris, 174
Newfoundland, 94
Newgate gaol, 41
Newton, Isaac, 160, 164, 169
Newton, John, 130
NHS and Welfare State, 23, 208
Nicholas Nickleby, 89
NME (New Musical Express), 151
No Name, 77
Nostromo, 55, 75
Oasis, 134
Ocean, Billy, 148
O'Connor, Sinead, 151
Octopussy, 52
Odell, Jack, 228
Oh Boy!, 134
Old Bailey, 174
Old Contemptibles, 102
Old Montague St, 226
Oldham, Andrew 'Loog', 147
Oliver Twist, 88
Oliver!, 70, 134
Olney, Buckinghamshire, 131
On The Buses, 67
O'Neal, Shaquille, 113
O'Neill, Terry, 188
Opium, 35
Optics and astronomy, 160
Orb, The, 151
Orient Wharf, 209
Orton, Arthur, 176
Orwell, George (Eric Blair), 80
Our Mutual Friend, 89
Out of Step, 83
Owen, Wilfred, 87
Oxford University, 124, 168, 212
Page, Jimmy, 147
Palladio and Palladian style, 170
Palmer, Samuel, 198
Pankhurst, Sylvia, Emmeline, Christabel, 30
Panopticon, 17

Paradise Row, 120
Paragon Theatre, Mile End Road, 58
Paramor, Norrie, 143
Parker, Charlie, 136
Parkhurst prison, 47
Paul Raymond Revuebar, 218
Pavilion Theatre, 36, 56
Peabody Buildings, 215
Peabody, George, 214
Peers Family, 223
Pennyfields, 80
People's Library, 77
People's Palace, Mile End, 76, 190
Pepys, Samuel, 78, 156, 181
'Peter the Painter', 18
Petrolle, Billy, 121
Petticoat Lane, 53
Petty, William, 169
Photographers, 188
Picture Post, 83
Pilgrim's Progress, 144
Plant, Robert, 147
Platt, Sir Hugh, 158
Poor Law, 17
Poplar, 80, 155
Poplar Workhouse, 10
Poplarism, 10, 25
Pound, Ezra, 87
Power, Nelly, 65
Prelleur, Peter (Pierre), 138
Pre-Raphaelite Brotherhood, 194
Presley, Elvis, 142
Primal Scream, 151
Prince Philip, 106
Prostitution, 126, 178
Public Image Ltd (PIL), 150
Pyment, Jim, 201
QPR, 115
Quakers (Society of Friends), 96, 207
Quasimodo, 71
Queen Anne, 20
Queen's Hall, Mile End, 190
Rabbi and Daughter, 193
Railway Tavern, Limehouse, 184
Raine's Foundation School, 53, 136
Raise the Titanic, 219
Raleigh, Sir Walter, 94
Ramsey MacDonald, 11
Raphael, 195
Ratcliff, 178
Ray, Johnny, 219
Reader's Digest, 199
Red Light Spells Danger, 148
Red Lion Street, 16
Redding, Otis, 135
Regent Street Polytechnic, 192
Regent's Canal, 162
Rennie, John, 166
Restoration, The, 79
Reynolds, Sir Joshua, 195
Richard II, 53
Richard, Cliff, 70, 142, 227
Rio de Janeiro, 176
River Lea/Lee, 222, 228
River Thames, 116, 154, 156
Robinson, Smokey, 135
Rock With the Caveman, 70
Rocker, Rudolf, 24
Rohmer, Sax, 34
Rolling Stones, 157, 189
Romeo and Juliet, 60
Rose Lane, 138
Rosenberg, Isaac, 86
Rossetti, Dante Gabriel and Christina, 194

232

INDEX

Rothenstein, Sir William, 192
Royal Academy, 190, 194
Royal College of Surgeons, 202
Royal Navy and pressganging, 97, 130, 159, 228
Royal Society, 97, 160, 165
Rudd, Martha, 76
Rumours, 141
Ruskin, John, 195, 200
Ryder, Sir William, 181
Saperstein, Abe, 112
Saskatoon, 100
Sassoon, Siegfried, 87
Savoy Big Five, 112
Savoy, The, 226
Scapa Flow, 98
School/Guild of Handicraft, 200
Scott, Ronnie (Schatt), 136, 227
Scurvy, 159
Seaside piers, 162
Sedaka, Neil, 143
Sellers, Peter, 120
Sex Pistols, 150
Sha La La La Lee, 134
Shadows, The, 140
Shadwell, 89, 125, 175
Shakespeare, William, 53, 60, 69
Shamen, The, 151
Shapiro, Helen, 142
Sharp, Cecil, 201
Sharp, Granville, 206
Shaw, Artie, 137
Shaw, George Bernard, 201
She Sits Among the Cabbages and Peas, 65
Shea, Frances, 189
Sheppard, Jack, 40
Sheringham, Teddy, 115
Shoreditch, 60, 67, 162, 224
Should Husbands Work, 59
Shrimpton, Jean, 189
Sidney Street Siege, 18, 46
Sims, Zoot, 137
Sinatra, Frank, 226
Sink the Belgrano, 53
Slack, Jack, 119
Slavery, 131, 206
Small Faces, 134
Smith, Leslie and Ronald, 228
Social Democratic Federation, 10
Society for the Abolition of the Slave Trade, 207
Soho, 166, 218
Somersett Ruling, 207
Somersett, James, 207
Sommers, Will, 61
Southend-on-Sea, 67
Southern (football) League, 110, 114
Southwark Bridge, 167
Spencer, Gabriel, 61
Spinks, Terry, 106
Spitalfields, 16, 20, 26, 40, 84, 125, 138, 165, 171, 192, 224
Spitalfields Mathematical Society, 164
Spot, Jack (Colmore, Comer, Camacho), 48
'SS Bella', 176
St Alban's Church, Wood St, 138
St Anne's Church, 171
St Dunstan's, Stepney, 97
St George's Church, 171
St John's, Vincent St, 211
St Leonard's Church, Shoreditch, 61
St Martin's School of Art, 70, 202

St Mary Woolnoth, City of London, 131
St Paul's Cathedral, 170
St Paul's School, 212
Stage, screen, cinema, 50-71
Stalin, 19
Steele, Tommy, 70
Stepney, 28, 46, 52, 68, 86, 97, 134, 171, 178, 180, 188
Stewart, Rod, 140
Stock Exchange (London), 165
Storm, Rory, 142
Stracey, John H, 189
Stratford, 223
Strong, Jonathan, 206
Sturm und Drang, 53
Suffrage (women's), 11, 30
Sun Yat-Sen, 101
Sunday Times, The, 189
Sutherland, Graham, 198
Swedenborg Square (Prince's Square), 129
Swedenborg, Emmanuel, 128
Swedish Church, Prince's Square, 128
Sweet Georgia Brown, 113
Swift, Jonathan, 21
Tahiti, 97
Taiwan, 101
Taylor, AJP, 10
Tennyson, Alfred Lord, 84
Thames Ironworks, 110
Thames TV, 219
That Was The Week That Was, 145
Road to Wigan Pier, The, 81
Secret Agent, The, 75
Shield, The 155
Sweeney, The, 63
'The Thunderer', 111
Trial, The, 52
Uncommercial Traveller, The, 89
'The Warrior', 110
Woman in White, The, 77
Theatre Royal, Stratford, 196
There'll Be Sad Songs to Make You Cry, 148
This Happy Breed, 54
Tichborne Claimant, 176
Tichborne, Lady Henrietta, 177
Tichborne, Sir Alfred, 176
Tichborne, Sir Roger Doughty, 176
Tilbury, 117, 154
Time Gentlemen Please!, 83
Titbits, 75
Titus Andronicus, 60
Toc H, 212
Top of the Pops, 148
Tottenham Outrage, 18
Tower Bridge, 154
Tower Hill, 28, 95, 213
Tower of London, 29, 95
Tower Subway, 197
Toynbee Hall, 22, 200
Trade unionism and strikes, 27
Trains and railway lines, 42
Trotsky, 19
Troxy Cinema, Poplar, 53
Turner, JMW, 195
Tusk, 141
Twang!, 71
Twiggy, 189
Two Lovely Black Eyes, 58
Tyburn gallows, 41
Tyson, Mike, 120
U2, 151
UEFA Cup, 115

Under Western Eyes, 75
Underwood St, 208
University College London, 16
Uppsala and Cathedral, 128
Upton Park, 111
US Congressional Medal, 215
US Declaration of Independence, 221
Utilitarianism, 16
Uxbridge, 183
Vanbrugh, John, 170
Variety Jubilee, 59
Varney, Reg, 66
Vaughan Williams, Ralph, 201
Victoria Cross, 99
Victoria Park, 53, 109
Victoria, Queen, 191
Vincent, Gene, 142, 146
Visions of You, 151
Wainwright, Henry, 36
Wales, Rosie, 103
Walking Back to Happiness, 142
Wallis, John, 169
Wally Pone of Soho, 71
Wapping, 54, 96, 125, 128, 130, 157, 159, 167, 171, 178, 206, 209
Ward, Seth, 169
Warner, Jack (Waters), 62
Waterloo Bridge, 167
Waterman's Arms, 82
Watermen, 116
Waters, Elsie and Doris (Gert and Daisy), 62
Waters, Muddy, 140
Watney St, 208
Watt, James, 166
Webber, Chris, 113
Webster, Ben, 137
Wedgewood, 145
Wedgewood, Josiah, 207
Wellclose Square, 128
Wellington, Duke of, 161
Wembley Stadium, 113
Wesley, Charles, 124
Wesley, John, 124, 131, 207
West Ferry Road, 114
West Ham, 156
West Ham Utd, 56, 110, 115, 120
Westminster Abbey, 89, 119, 215
Westminster School, 168
Wheeler's, Old Compton St, 197
When the Going Gets Tough, 148
Whitby, 96
Whitechapel , 37, 48, 71, 74, 78, 100, 112, 136, 144, 199, 200, 202, 208, 226
Wilberforce, William, 131, 207
Wilde, Oscar, 35
Wilkins, John, 169
Willis, Ted (Lord Willis), 63
Willis, Thomas, 169
Winston, Jimmy, 135
Wobble, Jah (John Wardle), 150
Wolsey, Cardinal 28
Woodford, 184
Workhouses, 23, 40, 175
World War I (The Great War, First World War), 35, 66, 86, 98, 102, 224
World War II (Second World War), 13, 203, 204, 225, 228
Wren, Sir Christopher, 168, 171
Yardbirds, The, 147
'Yellow Peril', 35
York Hall, 121
Young, Lester, 136
Zangwill, Israel, 90
Zionism, 91